The Disappearance of Morgan Nick

Kristin Samantha Morton

Published by Trellis Publishing, 2021.

While every precaution has been taken in the preparation of this book, the publisher assumes no responsibility for errors or omissions, or for damages resulting from the use of the information contained herein.

THE DISAPPEARANCE OF MORGAN NICK

First edition. July 13, 2021.

Copyright © 2021 Kristin Samantha Morton.

ISBN: 979-8224950324

Written by Kristin Samantha Morton.

The Disappearance of Morgan Nick

Kristin Samantha Morton

1

Excitement filled the air in Alma, Arkansas on the night of June 9, 1995. A crowd of nearly three hundred surrounded the baseball pitch to watch a little league game on a warm summer night. Cheering could be heard echoing around the town, reaching far from the stadium. In what appeared to be a perfect summer's evening, spirits were high, with adults chatting jovially and children playing together, making new friends. But for one mother, the midsummer evening would become a living nightmare in an incident she would describe in an interview for Fox News as "pure childhood innocence and such evil that met in [the] same moment." Her six-year-old daughter disappeared, never to be seen or heard from again.

Morgan Chauntel Nick was the eldest daughter to Colleen and John Nick. Born on September 12, 1988, Morgan grew up happily in Ozark, Arkansas, a small community with fewer than four thousand residents. She was six years old in 1995, by which age she was showing promising signs for a bright future. Her aspirations were to become a doctor or a circus performer. A loving girl, Morgan adored her adopted pet kitten, Emily, and enjoyed playing with her brother, Logan, and baby sister, Taryn. But she also still had characteristics typical of a young girl. She was very shy around strangers and had a fear of the dark. Her mother tried to encourage her to join her school's track team, but Morgan quickly protested when she realised that running outside was tiring and made her sweat. Instead, she joined her local Girl Scouts group, preferring to stay indoors and doing crafts.

On June 9, 1995, Colleen and Morgan decided to drive to the nearby town of Alma for the evening to watch a little league baseball game and spend some quality time together. The mother and daughter had not spent one-on-one time together for a long while, so they thought this would be the perfect opportunity to hang out, just the two of them. In an interview for *Unsolved Mysteries*, Colleen stated, "We'd made the choice to go, just Morgan and I, just to have [a] girls' night out, and it was just such a warm, close, fun night." Morgan was in a playful mood, making a game out of regularly untying her mother's shoes. She soon became friendly with two other children from Alma, Jessica and Tye, and at about 10.30pm, the three youngsters asked Morgan's mother if they could leave the bleachers to go and play. Colleen was initially hesitant due to the late hour and being unfamiliar with the area they were in. Reassured by surrounding parents that the area was safe, and ultimately bending to her daughter's irresistible pleas, she agreed. There was only fifteen minutes left in the game, so what harm could come to her daughter in such a busy, well-lit area?

After giving her mother a big hug and a kiss on the cheek, Morgan and her two new friends ran off in single file uphill toward the nearby parking lot with the intention of catching fireflies. The area was illuminated by lampposts in the car park, and when Colleen turned to look, she could see Morgan in her green Girl Scout t-shirt, blue denim shorts, and white leather sneakers, playing happily with the two other children just fifty yards away. Tye would state in an interview twenty years later, "If you were a kid and you were at the baseball field, you always wanted to be at the top of the hill 'cause ... you could see everything." There was also a large sand pile at the top of the hill, set aside for impending construction nearby. Ignoring its weird smell, the local children would play in the sand, just as Tye, Jessica and Morgan did that evening. As the game neared its end, the children decided to empty the sand from their shoes before returning to their parents. Jessica and Tye sat on the front of a car bonnet to get their shoes off, while Morgan was at the back. Just after 10.45pm, as the baseball game finished, Jessica and Tye ran to the bottom of the hill, only to realise that Morgan wasn't with them. Colleen questioned the children about Morgan's whereabouts, and they all assumed Morgan was still at the top of the hill in the parking lot, waiting by her mother's car. As the crowd began to make their way from the baseball field to their cars, Colleen ran to her own vehicle only to discover Morgan wasn't waiting beside it. She searched frantically all around the car, even looking in the back seat, thinking her eldest daughter might have gotten in. But it soon became chillingly clear that Morgan wasn't there, and as the car park emptied of people, the horrifying truth hit Colleen: her daughter was missing. Years later, Jessica would fight back tears while telling Fox News, "It's just a terrible situation and if I just would've stopped or we would've stayed together better, then it wouldn't have ever happened."

Noticing Colleen was in distress, a baseball coach approached her to ask what had happened. Upon hearing that Colleen's six-year-old daughter had vanished, the coach quickly turned to question the two children Morgan had been playing with. The situation would become even more disturbing as Jessica and Tye revealed that a man they described as "creepy" looking had been watching them as they played and even spoke to Morgan as she stood by the back of the car, putting her shoes back on. Realising the severity of the situation, the baseball coach used his cellphone to call the police who arrived on the scene approximately six minutes later to begin their investigation, but they found no trace of Morgan. With no immediate clues, the police had to rely on heavy media coverage and poster distribution to encourage witnesses to come forward. Their highest priority soon became to identify and find the man the children had described to the baseball coach. As news of Morgan's disappearance spread, it became distressingly clear that Jessica and Tye hadn't been the only people at the game to witness the man observing the children.

Following their initial appeal for information, the police received an overwhelming number of tips and leads to consider. They questioned all three hundred people who had attended the baseball game on June 9, and a number of witnesses commented upon the strange looking man who stood watching the children as they played. With Alma being such a tight-knit community, it was assumed that he was most likely a visitor from out of town, but familiar enough with the area to know where to find children if he was, in fact, a predator. Believed to be between twenty-three and thirty-eight years of age, he was described as a white male, approximately six feet tall and of a medium build, and spoke with a "hillbilly" accent. His hair was slightly curly and black with distinct salt-and-pepper colouring, and he wore it combed back. He also had a moustache and beard which suggested he hadn't shaved in roughly three to four days. It was a warm night, and he wore nothing but blue cut-off jean shorts, walking barefoot with his chest hair on show. Although his behaviour struck some as unusual, nobody considered his dress to be too out of the ordinary on such a warm night. Jessica told Fox News in 2015, "At eight, you don't expect somebody to do anything. We're around adults all the time, I wasn't scared of anybody. I mean, it was a little strange, but you're innocent at that point. You don't think something like that is ever gonna happen." But youthful naivety and the trusting nature of a small town would soon be shattered for many in Alma and the wider Arkansas state, leaving many horrified that such a disturbing crime could take place in brightly lit conditions so close to hundreds of witnesses.

Witnesses also clearly described a vehicle that the man appeared to be driving, parked near the car park where Morgan was last seen. It was a red Ford pickup with a white camper shell, the paint of the car dulled by age. There was noticeable damage to the camper shell on the right at the rear, and it was described as being a few inches too short for the truck, not fitting properly. Although the man wasn't known in Alma, his truck appeared to have Arkansas license plates. Despite no one seeing this man take Morgan, many find it coincidental that his truck was gone when Colleen, Jessica, and Tye returned to the top of the hill to search for the six-year-old girl. Tye would state in 2015, "I didn't see him pick her up and take her, but there's just no other way ... he was up there when we left, but he was gone when we got back. So was she." Although Tye and Jessica heard the man speaking with Morgan, the details of their conversation have never been publicly disclosed, as investigators consider this to be the main piece of specific knowledge they have that could help screen out false confessions, but also one day catch the culprit.

A composite sketch of this unknown man was drawn and released to the public. It received wide media coverage across the state of Arkansas, and authorities consequently received four thousand tips. Upon further investigation, it was uncovered that an unknown man had attempted to lure a four-year-old into his red truck at a laundromat earlier in the same day, June 9. Fortunately, the child's mother spotted the man, and stopped her child going any further, drawing attention to the predator who quickly sped off. The similarities in description and crime are uncanny, but it remains unclear if the man at the laundry was responsible for Morgan's kidnapping. The day after Morgan's abduction, police received another report from Fort Smith, Arkansas, just fifteen miles away from Alma. A male had tried to coax a nine-year-old girl into a men's restroom inside a convenience store. This proved to be another unsuccessful attempt by a predator, but the key coincidence was that the man – once again unnamed – matched the description of the man who reportedly took Morgan. The legitimacy of these claims has been hotly debated on recent blog and forum posts by online crime sleuths, with some going so far as to dismiss the two reports of attempted abduction altogether. While being their lead suspect, the man who kidnapped Morgan is yet to be identified and tracked down. Speaking on the twentieth anniversary of Morgan's disappearance, Alma Police Chief Russell White publicly stated that the culprit "is probably a person by nature who is a loner, had very few friends. He committed a crime and has not told anybody."

Colleen Nick refused to leave Alma after the incident, part in fear that she would be leaving her daughter behind, part in hope that her daughter would be found somewhere in the small town. For six weeks, she lived in a volunteer fire station neighbouring the police station, and became a key figure leading searches and printing and posting flyers around the area. Hope has been a primary driving force for Colleen ever since her daughter went missing, and she stated, "I believe and I hope every single day that I get up, that today is the day that Morgan comes home. And every night when I go to bed and she's not back yet, I know that I'm one day closer to getting her back." But it has been a difficult journey for the Nick family. Upon finally returning home to Ozark after her initial six week stay in Alma, Colleen and her now ex-husband, John, faced the difficult task of trying to explain events to their two youngest children, then aged four and twenty-two months. Too young to fully comprehend the situation, four-year-old Logan, missing his playmate Morgan, would regularly scold his tearful mother for losing his big sister. These children grew to realise the severity of the situation with every year that passed, snatching their innocence away at a heartbreakingly young age.

Paranoia swept Alma for years after the event, with the town's residents becoming much more vigilant in their actions. Doors were locked in neighbourhoods where they had once been left wide open. Parents worried about leaving their children to play unattended in the park or in their backyards. But the small town did not let the incident tear them down. Instead, they banded together to support Colleen and her two younger children in their search for Morgan. Together, the local communities and the FBI offered a total reward of $60,000 for the recovery of Morgan, as well as the identification, arrest, and conviction of those responsible for her disappearance. Two years after Morgan's disappearance, Colleen took her two younger children, Logan and Taryn, and moved to Alma to be closer to the root of the investigation, buying the only house she was able to afford. Every year, the entire family meets on June 9th to remember Morgan, and release balloons tagged with a photograph of her and an information card — one balloon for each day she has been missing. It has become an entire community event, with hundreds of thousands of balloons being sent off into the sky at the site Morgan was last seen.

When news of Morgan's abduction first broke, public reaction was astonishing, with hundreds volunteering time, efforts, and funds in an effort to help find the missing girl or her kidnapper. The mass investigation which took place immediately after June 9 provided thousands of leads, and Alma Police Department had to dedicate an entire room filled with new filing cabinets to the Morgan Nick case, which still stands today, with new tips continuing to be investigated and stored. The state-wide amber emergency alert in Arkansas was also renamed shortly after Morgan's disappearance, continuing to be known as the 'Morgan Nick Amber Alert' to this day. Using this emergency broadcast system, warnings would be sent to police departments across the state as well as two hundred and fifty radio stations whenever a child under the age of twelve is abducted or goes missing.

A year after Morgan's abduction, Colleen established the Morgan Nick Foundation, a non-profit organisation which seeks to support the parents of missing children, as well as providing education to help prevent children from being taken by predators. Colleen noted that there was no structured support network in place for her following the abduction of Morgan. With almost two thousand children going missing in the United States every day, a statistic which holds true today, Colleen wanted to ensure there was a central organisation that would continue to fight for the safety of children and their families while giving her the resources to continue her search for her own daughter. The Morgan Nick Foundation strives to intervene in missing children cases, providing families with a safe environment and strong network of rescue workers and resources, whilst also passing vital information directly on to law enforcement, acting as an official liaison. It also provides free educational services to families, police, and youth leadership to teach both children and adults about safety skills and abduction prevention, striving to protect children from the dangers of abduction and exploitation. As of 2010, Colleen had assisted in reuniting over one hundred children with their families through her work at the Foundation and the Centre for Missing and Exploited Children. Between 2010 and 2015, the Foundation aided in recovering forty children who had been missing for more than twenty years, furthering Colleen's belief that Morgan could still feasibly be found. Her belief that Morgan might one day come home is the key driving force behind her continued efforts to prevent future cases of child abduction, "If I quit fighting for her, eventually everyone else will quit fighting for her as well."

The case gained considerable traction in 2001 when an updated composite sketch was released, revealing how her assumed abductor may look, as well as a new sketch of how Morgan may look aged twelve. In August of the same year, popular TV show *Unsolved Mysteries* released an episode highlighting Morgan's disappearance. With the case back in the public eye, investigators were overwhelmed with new sources of information and potential leads. One tip was deemed "so specific" that police arranged to conduct a dig on private land in Booneville, Arkansas. On January 15, 2002, the authorities arrived with police dogs and spent the day digging in search of Morgan's body. The search of the land continued until approximately 9.30pm, but unfortunately no evidence was uncovered, and police stated that they did not intend to return to the area to search further.

On the tenth anniversary of Morgan's disappearance, the local community nominated the Nick family to participate in the show, *Extreme Home Makeovers*. This special two-hour episode saw the townspeople of Alma come together to help rebuild the Nicks' modest home into a large, welcoming environment where Colleen could continue to work, whilst spending cherished quality time with Logan and Taryn. The team created a bedroom for Morgan, in hope she would one day return, and placed a custom porchlight by the front door to help guide her home, specially engraved with "love always hopes". The special was not only dedicated to building the Nicks a new, special home, but also to raise awareness of child abduction in America. The hosts of the show raised a billboard on a busy interstate just outside of Alma, knowing that nearly eighty thousand cars pass the area every day. On the billboard was a photograph of Morgan aged six, and a reconstruction of how she might look at age sixteen, helping to expose the story to a wider audience in hope it would trigger a memory in somebody. The *Extreme Home Makeovers* team also worked with the Morgan Nick Foundation and the Center for Missing and Exploited Children to provide free photographing and fingerprinting of all the children in the local community.

Hope returned on November 16, 2010, when Crawford County investigators received a tip from a narcotics officer based in Spiro, Oklahoma, just thirty-five miles from Alma. They were notified about a vacant trailer which had been home to a man convicted of child molestation and rape who was serving time in Oklahoma penitentiary at time of the alert. The convict in question had been considered a person of interest since Morgan went missing and had never been ruled out of the case, as the police were never able to fully dismiss his potential involvement. Detectives from Crawford County travelled to Spiro to assist in the investigation in the hope of uncovering traces of Morgan's DNA, but couldn't find any evidence that Morgan had been in the home. The man who owned the trailer in 2010 was also questioned in connection to Morgan's case, but gave the police no new leads. However, in December 2017, the authorities would return to the area, now owned by new owners unconnected to Morgan's disappearance. A new tip had been received, suggesting that there may be a hidden well somewhere on the property. Investigators arrived at the scene with cadaver dogs, telling reporters on the scene that this location was considered the "center of the investigation". The land was diligently searched, with officers digging only one inch at a time to allow the Oklahoma Medical Examiner's Office time to carefully look at every piece of stone and soil being moved. The dig continued well into the early evening, but as the diggers reached approximately two feet in depth, they hit solid bedrock, ultimately indicating that there was no well near the site. The search in Spiro once again proved fruitless and was called off the next day with no new evidence being unearthed.

To compound the horror of the case came opportunists looking to exploit the missing girl's identity. In June 2012, 24-year-old Tonya Smith from Hollister, Missouri, attempted to assume Morgan's identity. Using the website VitalCheck, Tonya purchased personal documents and a birth certificate using Morgan's personal information. As Morgan's case was high profile, police were immediately alerted. Colleen was also aware of the alert and was devastated to discover it wasn't her daughter behind the computer keyboard, but someone looking to use their tragedy for her own gain. Speaking publicly at the time of the case, Colleen stated, "I'm really angry someone would try to steal Morgan's identity. That they would have the nerve to try and steal from her the one thing she has left, and that's who she is." The police were all too familiar with the dreadful motivations behind stealing a child's identity for fraud, knowing that people who are trying to avoid detection but wanting to get paid employment often target the identity of youngsters. These cases often go undetected, as children aren't usually subjected to credit checks, however this was one of the first times anyone had tried to abuse a missing child's identity. Authorities searched three states for the culprit, and Tonya was finally apprehended and arrested for computer fraud on August 2, 2012, in Branson, Missouri, spending one hundred and twenty days in Pulaski County Jail before her trial. On February 28, 2013, Tonya was sentenced to six years of probation and was required to pay a $2,500 fine.

As of this year, Morgan has been missing for twenty-three years, but the case is far from cold. Tips have continued to pour in across the two decades since she vanished. The authorities involved in inspecting the disappearance admit that there is considerable difficulty in working on a case like this, particularly as there was no physical evidence left at the scene of the crime or later uncovered by a lead, and because there were no eye-witnesses who saw somebody take Morgan to fully confirm their suspicions. In 2010, Alma Police Chief Russell White claimed, "What makes it a hard case to crack is that it's a real simple crime. It's not a conspiracy and does not involve a lot of people." If they are to ever solve this case, it is vital that a reliable tip is provided.

Tragically, Morgan Nick remains missing and has not been seen or heard from since that fateful evening at the little league baseball game in the summer of 1995. For Morgan's family, days suddenly became years, but they have never given up hope. Colleen and John eventually separated, but each continue to search for their missing daughter. Their devotion to finding their daughter has been to the benefit of the state of Arkansas, with the establishment of a new foundation dedicated to finding missing children, supporting grieving families, and educating the community. It's a dedication that has to be admired, and is best reflected in a public, heartfelt letter that Colleen and John shared on the Morgan Nick Foundation website:

"Dear Morgan,

We want you to know how special you are! You are a blessing we cannot live without. We feel cheated every day that goes by and we do not see your smile, hear your bubbly laughter [or] listen to your thoughts and ideas. We have never stopped believing that we'll find you. We are saving all our hugs and kisses for you. Always know that you are loved.

Most of all, don't ever give up.

We WILL find you. We promise!

Love,

Mom & Dad."

MISSING BETHANY: THE TRUE STORY OF BETHANY DECKER

13

JENNY GREENWOOD

In many ways the life of Bethany Decker was not so different from others her age and who shared similar backgrounds. She worked full time as a waitress and attended college at George Mason University, majoring in Global Environmental Change. Sure, she was only 22 and married with one son, just 17-months-old. But that is hardly uncommon. And yes, her marriage was faltering, but even that was hardly unique, especially when married at such a young age to a husband serving repeated tours of duty in Afghanistan.

Nothing about Bethany seemed out of the ordinary.

Until she disappeared.

On January 29th, 2011 the young wife and mother vanished and has not been seen since.

What happened to Bethany Decker?

At the time of her disappearance, Bethany and her husband, Emile Decker had been married for 18 months. Their son was living with Bethany's mother, Kim Nelson, while Bethany focused on finishing her last semester at George Mason.

"She is my flip flops and lip gloss girl," her mother said, giving her that nickname because she was born in Hawaii. Bethany was a terrific student and graduated from high school with a 4.0 GPA. At the time of her disappearance she was only just a few credits shy of graduating from George Mason University. Her studies by day and her hard work as a waitress by night was about to pay off. With her degree she hoped to change the world in a positive way.

"Bethany was a physically attractive young woman," forensic psychologist Tim McGee said. "She was petite at four-foot-eleven and weighed 130 pounds. She was curvy and had a pretty face. Surely, she had more than her share of men who wanted to date her. Invariably, she attracted men who would be uncomfortable with dating someone who got a lot of attention from rivals."

As days and weeks passed with no contact, her family said they didn't begin to worry right away since the 21-year-old had such a hectic schedule. With Bethany away at college and working full-time it had not concerned her mother that she had not heard from her daughter in over three weeks. She tried calling on several occasions and was just directed to her voice-mail box.

"She had a seventeen-month old child at the time," McGee said. "But the child would stay with her in-laws. Still, those days where no one heard from her would suggest that they were used to not having her checking-in. So there is the possibility that there was some estrangement there."

Kim Nelson was not the only one struggling to get a hold of Bethany. One weekend Kim received a number of strange phone calls and some of Bethany's friends noticed unusual posts on Bethany's Facebook page.

"It was a Saturday morning and I had messages from four different people from different parts of the country that said, 'there's somebody on Facebook that's on Bethany's login, but it's not Bethany. It didn't sound like Bethany and didn't use terms Bethany would use. What's going on? Is there something wrong?'" Bethany's mother Kim said.

Kim immediately called her own parents to check on Bethany because they lived closer to her apartment in Ashburn, Virginia. Upon arrival, they noticed that Bethany's car was parked crooked, had a flat tire, and was dusty. This was peculiar because her grandparents drove past only one week prior and the car was parked differently.

The unused car, the Facebook posts, and the radio silence from Bethany formed mounting evidence that something was not quite right. But what finally inspired her family to call the police was when her grandparents knocked on her door and heard no answer.

"We just had a feeling. We were concerned," Evelyn Bayles, Bethany's grandmother said.

On February 19, 2011 Bayles called the local police dept. and investigators soon descended upon the apartment complex and interviewed every collateral contact in Bethany's life. But it had been at least three weeks since anyone had seen her. The only trace left behind was her dusty, double-parked car.

The vehicle was searched, but it left no clues as to where she might have disappeared to. Her apartment revealed nothing. It was entirely empty, except for a bag of her own clothes. There were no signs of foul play or a physical altercation. Her bank account had been static for weeks. Soon, the police organized search teams who prowled the nearby landscape with dogs and combed through dumpsters, looking for human remains. She had not shown up for her scheduled shift at Carrabba's Italian Grill in Centreville, VA, the popular restaurant chain where she worked, since the day she was last seen. She had disappeared without a trace.

"We want Bethany safe. We love her and we want to know that she is OK," Bethany's mother said to reporters. An investigator also noted that there was no evidence or indication that Bethany was not alive. But behind the investigator's affirmation, lay the disturbing truth that there was no activity on her bank account, email account, or cell phone records.

SUSPECT THE HUSBAND FIRST

At first, the disappearance seemed like an elaborate ruse engineered by Bethany's husband, Emile. According to police, Emile had seen Bethany the day before she disappeared. And despite finding no activity on her bank account, email account, or cell phone records, someone was still posting on her Facebook account.

Someone had her login information. Who better to suspect than her husband?

The investigators started to circle their wagons around Emile. The motive lined up all-too-well. He was a young man stuck serving in Afghanistan while quietly harboring suspicions that Bethany was being unfaithful. She had become pregnant again but was it even his child? One week before her disappearance, between Jan. 18 to Jan. 23, Bethany and Emile had vacationed in Hawaii in what was possibly a desperate last-ditch attempt to save their marriage. When that failed, the investigators speculated, Emile descended into a fit of rage and Bethany disappeared.

What buttressed this theory was that she was never at the airport to bid him farewell before he returned to Afghanistan on February 2nd 2011. His wife did not see him off, as she had multiple times before, investigators said. His fellow infantrymen thought this was peculiar but attributed it to the marital difficulties that Emile was experiencing.

Armed with this information, investigators were eager to interrogate Emile and did so within a few days of Bethany's disappearance.

"He is cooperating. He's answered several questions for us now," a spokesman for the police said. They did not have details of their conversation with Emile, but said they were trying to establish a more solid time line of when Bethany was last seen based on information from her husband.

But because Emile was serving in Afghanistan by the time the investigation started, investigators needed to contact U.S. military officials to arrange bringing him back home for further questioning and a polygraph test.

But Emile was not being named a suspect or a person of interest in the case.

"I don't want to limit him saying he's a suspect or a person of interest at this time. We're playing catch up on an investigation of a missing person, therefore, we would like to talk to as many people as possible," the police spokesman said.

"He wants to cooperate fully. He was very concerned of Bethany's whereabouts and condition. Obviously, being the father of their child he wants to hear a good resolution to this."

AN AFFAIR AT WORK

Bethany was having an affair with a man named Ronald Roldan, a Bolivian immigrant she met at Carrabba's Italian Grill. With that information, it wasn't inconceivable that the five-months pregnant Bethany was carrying Roldan's child. Investigators now had someone other than Emile with a possible motive in the case.

Roldan would also be the last person to see her in the Ashburn apartment on January 29th, 2011.

The two were reportedly living together in the Orchard Grass Terrace complex until the lease expired on Jan. 31, and from the very beginning, according to friends and family, the relationship was abusive. Bethany Decker met Roldan at a vulnerable time in her life according to her mother. She did not plan on being in a relationship with Roldan, nor staying in a relationship with him. When Nelson first met him, she found him to be charming. But friends and family soon learned that he turned controlling and even dangerous. Friends insisted that she check-in regularly with them as the relationship turned from emotionally abusive to physically abusive.

"The whole circumstance of her getting involved with Roldan is nuts," McGee said. "The media had to be careful not to judge her for behavior in having an affair because then that suggests that she brought on the violence to herself. But it is apparent that her mother knew about the affair."

Bethany had been desperately exploring a safe exit strategy from the relationship, according to her mother. But Roldan refused to leave and he would not let her leave either. She confided to her mother the danger that Roldan posed to her life, saying there was a time when Roldan threw her across the room and into a wall. He threatened to cut her open with car keys. Her family encouraged her to just walk away from the relationship, but she insisted that, "He'll never let it go. He'll find me."

Investigators believe that Bethany was in the Ashburn apartment the day she went missing because she made a commitment to work that evening at Carrabba's Italian Grill, not far away from Ashburn. But she never showed up for her scheduled shift, thus making Roldan the last person to see her that day.

In March 2011, only a few weeks after the initial investigation was launched, investigators searched Roldan's family home, where he was living with his mother and seized his immigration papers, a black bag with assorted documents, and other items, according to a search warrant filed in Fairfax County.

As the investigation progressed, investigators told reporters at the time that Roldan "made conflicting statements regarding when he noticed Bethany's car being parking in the parking lot in front of their shared apartment." Eventually, at some point during the investigation, detectives said Roldan stopped cooperating with law enforcement.

"Some are cooperative, some are not. We feel we have probably interviewed folks in this investigation already that probably have information that we would like to have and they've been reluctant to hand that information over. So, we're hopeful that, as the days go by, that they'll realize that if they have information, no matter how insignificant they think it is, they will give it to us," former Sheriff Steve Simpson told reporters in 2011. Bethany's mother, Nelson, believes that Sheriff Simpson was likely referring to Roldan's family members who were holding back on sharing pertinent information.

As investigators dug deeper into Roldan's past they found a violent criminal record that aligned perfectly with the alleged abuse in his relationship with Bethany. In one incident he smashed a woman's car windshield in a fit of rage. According to investigators, when they interviewed Roldan's other girlfriends prior to Bethany, he demonstrated a clear pattern of abuse.

On Friday, Aug. 5, 2011, the Loudoun County investigators released new photos of Bethany, hoping the images would generate new information as to her whereabouts. They clearly had not yet given up hope that she was still alive.

Bethany was due to give birth to her second child on Sunday, Aug. 7, and hope remained that somewhere, some hospital would recognize her if she were seeking medical treatment. "We're trying to get the picture out as to how she would look today," said a spokesman for the sheriff's office.

The photos released to the media showed Bethany when she was in the final trimester of pregnancy with her first child. A second photo showed an image of a tattoo just above her left ankle. For investigators, it was still the only path forward. "Nothing has led us in any other direction," an investigator said.

The investigation turned cold from there. It was clear that Bethany wasn't coming back. She was likely dead. Weeks turned into months and months into years. There were no new leads and no sign of Bethany. It was not until 2014 that the case took an important twist-perhaps the most shocking clue of all which would lead many to conclude that Roldan had in fact murdered her.

In 2014 Roldan had moved on to a new relationship with another young woman, Vicky Willoughby. The same pattern of abuse that happened in his relationship with Bethany, as alleged by her friends and family, would also emerged in his new relationship. Willoughby ultimately moved to a new city, Pinehurst, NC to escape from her relationship with Roldan, but he soon followed her.

Police responded to a 911 call for a domestic violence incident at 1:30 a.m. on Nov. 12, 2014. Willoughby had shot Roldan in self-defense twice — once in the chest and once in the abdomen. But the weak stopping power of her .38 caliber handgun did not bring him down. Instead, Roldan charged forward and wrestled the gun out of Willoughby's hand and shot her three times, hitting her in the head and leg. Miraculously, she survived the shooting, but lost her right eye.

Four months later, Roldan was charged with the attempted murder of Willoughby. In addition to shooting her, Roldan also broke Willoughby's neck, bit her, and punched her.

Roldan took a plea deal in the case in May, 2015 and the charges were consolidated into one sentence, with a minimum of six years and a maximum of eight years and three months. Roldan pleaded guilty to two reduced charges — felony assault with a deadly weapon with intent to kill, inflicting serious injury, and felony assault inflicting serious bodily injury.

But with time served, he could be released as early as 2020. The Assistant District Attorney in the case, Peter Strickland, said he made the decision to accept the plea agreement during jury selection.

Presumably, after he finishes his prison sentence, U.S. Immigration and Customs Enforcement would take custody of Roldan to begin processing him for deportation back to Bolivia. But with millions of criminally convicted immigrants awaiting deportation approval from their host countries, his future status in the U.S. remains unclear.

As for Willoughby, she was astonished that an attempted murder case such as this would yield such a light sentence.

"I am disappointed in the gaps leading to technicalities and diminishing the consequences for such violence," Willoughby said. "This was not a first offense. Violent repeat offenders should be kept off the street. I fear for the next victim, in this country or another."

The other offense Willoughby was referring to, of course, was Bethany's disappearance. His arrest and subsequent plea-deal triggered red flags for those still investigating Bethany's disappearance. His pattern of controlling, obsessive behavior with women was apparent. But now there was actual, documented evidence of his capacity to cross the line from obsessive, stalking behavior into dangerous violence.

Bethany's mother had hoped for a longer sentence for Roldan. "There is no sentence that can equate to the terror and suffering caused by Ronald to Vicky and others, including Bethany," she told reporters,

"I am hoping that him being behind bars will allow someone who has information about Bethany to come forward so there can be justice for Bethany. I pray that their heart would be moved to do the right thing so their [conscience will be] clear."

In cases such as these, prior convictions or arrests go a long way towards demonstrating an actual pattern of abuse. Most violent criminals have a long record of exhibiting violent behaviors and domestic abusers, in particular, have a history of controlling and obsessive behavior with their significant others, often punctuated by fits of rage and violence.

Domestic abuse is unlikely to end when the victim ends the relationship. In fact, it can often escalate when the abused victim tries to separate. The abusers will explode at the impending loss of control. Many murders of abused women occur during or after the separation, when the abuser feels the victim is escaping his control and he fails to re-establish it.

Research shows that the overwhelming number of domestic abusers are never arrested. Those that are arrested often had prior domestic violence arrests or orders of protection filed against them and fall into the category of serial domestic abusers. Additionally, only a very small percentage of those arrested for domestic violence had no prior criminal history at all.

Investigators never charged Roldan or named him as a suspect, but said he is no longer willing to answer questions about Bethany's disappearance and acknowledge that there are no other suspects. They also maintain that they have no evidence that suggests Decker is alive or dead.

One day after Roldan's guilty plea, on Friday, May 13, it was (or would have been) Bethany's 27th birthday. Nelson wished her daughter a happy birthday on her Facebook page and said, "We have been waiting a long time but will not lose hope."

Whether or not any further leads will develop in this case is unclear. But investigators, after five years, finally filed a search warrant requesting access to a cellphone, tablet and laptop belonging to Ronald Roldan. And buried within the search warrant, was a revealing quote from Roldan's ex-girlfriend, Willoughby, who told police Roldan once said, "I've made someone disappear before and I'll do it again."

So does the evidence implicate Roland in the disappearance and likely murder of Bethany Decker? Without actual forensic evidence or even definitive proof that she is dead, it is unlikely that any charges will be brought against Roldan. But what is almost certainly clear is that Roldan fit the pattern of a serial domestic abuser. The prior criminal convictions, the allegations of abuse from Bethany's family, and his refusal to submit to a polygraph test, makes him a a likely suspect in the court of public opinion.

MISSING MISTY

Misty Copsey was fourteen years old when she disappeared on September 17th, 1992 after a trip to the Puyallup Fair.

Her case remains a showcase of administrative screw-ups and dropped balls. She was initially thought of as a runaway before foul play was finally suspected a month after the fact. Subsequently, there have been at least five people suspected of committing her abduction.

But the Puyallup police did not get within sniffing distance of Misty or charging anyone with her disappearance. Three different police chiefs and numerous detectives all took a swing at the case and whiffed. No one in law enforcement has been able to answer the question on everyone's lips.

What happened to Misty Copsey?

A GOOD GIRL

Misty was born in 1978 to Diana and Paul "Buck" Copsey. Her father was a firefighter but the couple split up shortly after she was born and Misty lived with her mother.

Misty got good grades in school, excelling particularly in Math. During her last quarter at Spanaway Lake Junior High School, she got A's and B's. Athletic, she played softball, volleyball, and basketball before breaking both forearms during an athletic practice.

Misty was not the ringleader of a bad crowd. She was diffident but funny, entertaining her friends while skipping around and singing the theme song to Sesame Street.

She did not have much in regards to material wants. Her mother eked out a living as an in-home care nurse and they lived in a mobile home park until she was fourteen. Seeking a better place to live, Diana and Misty moved into a duplex where she now had her own room. But Misty longed for her friend who lived in and around the old trailer park. She would make it back there when she could to just hang out.

Tall, blonde and with green eyes, Misty was cute enough to draw the attention of boys. She remained chaste, however, and was not dating like so many of her other friends.

Her innocent, girl-next-door looks would draw the attention of Rheuban Schmidt. Rheuban looked like a casting call actor for a meth head. He sported a reverse mullet, a hairstyle that was cut close to the sides with curls on top. He had beady, green eyes that screamed low IQ. One of Misty's friends described him as a "scuzzy looking dude" but he nonetheless befriends Misty, much to the chagrin of her mother.

Diana grew suspicious of the relationship as Rheuban was four years older and a high school dropout. On one occasion, she listened in on the other end of a phone conversation Misty was having with Rheuban.

"I get horny just looking at you, Misty," Rheuban said, whispering like an old pervert.

Diana became enraged and ordered her daughter off the phone.

"Don't ever talk to that idiot again...."

ENTER CORY BOBER

Cory Bober was a thorn in the side of police every since the Green River killings became a national news story. He would insist that the police are "incompetent fools" while organizing his own searches for her remains. Diana would later accuse him of killing her daughter but he would respond by telling Diana that she was being "ungrateful." He was, after all, the only man on the case.

Bober was a recluse without a vehicle or a drive's license. An inveterate marijuana user, he had a record for both possession and dealing. He was also obsessed with cases of murdered or slain women in his home state of Washington. He had a stack of binders with autopsy reports, pictures, and other arcane details.

Bober came under the radar of the police in Puyallup when he became obsessed with the Green River Killer case. He had a brief acquaintance with Randall Dean Achziger, remembering a conversation where the man told him that the killer inserted rocks into the remains of his victim. Bober became suspicious as that would turn out to be a piece of information only known to police. He then went on a one-man crusade to prove the guilt of Achziger. Bober would interview his ex-girlfriends, friends, co-workers and present all of this in an affidavit to the courts.

Achziger found it ridiculous and annoying.

So did the police.

The Green River Killer would turn out to be a painter named Gary Leon Ridgway.

Bober didn't give up, however. He knew Achziger was the guy.

Bober had his own theories about who was performing the killings. Some were wild and outlandish conspiracy theories. Others were spot on. He would notice that there were victims that "had disappeared on the very same date that others were discovered. Some victims seemed to almost 'commemorate' the deaths or discoveries of others; one would die on a particular date and another would disappear a year to the day later on the very same date."

The police dismissed his theories as the rantings of a crack head. But Bober would be willing to show the proof of his connect the dots calculations. He pointed to the cases of Kim Delange, a 15-year-old killed in 1988 and Anna Chebetnoy, a 14-year-old killed in 1990. Both of their bodies would be found along Highway 410, east of Enumclaw.

Bober discovered that the remains of both girls were found in the same section of 410. The girls were found two years and one month apart. He felt that the killer was following a pattern.

He called the police department and left a voice mail. He predicted that a teen girl from Puyallup would disappear and her remains would be found on Highway 410 in the same vicinity where the other girl's bodies were found. Bober gave him the name of the man whom he felt was the serial killer.

Randall Achziger.

But the police were now used to his calls and viewed him as a crank. A nutcake with a strange vendetta.

His prediction would be half-right, however.

There would be no body found on Highway 410.

But a teenage girl would disappear.

Her name was Misty Copsey.

A NIGHT AT THE FAIR

On September 17th, 1992, Diana told her daughter Misty and her best friend Trina Bevard to behave themselves. Misty had convinced her mother to let them stay out that night...free of any meddlesome adults. But Trina's guardian would not allow her to go without an adult driving them home.

Diana worked as a caregiver for a 97-year-old Alzheimer patient who could not be left alone. She would not be able to drive the girls home. But Misty checked the bus schedules and convinced her mother that they would be okay. There was a bus that left the fair at 8:40 p.m.

Misty then convinced her mother to lie to Trina's guardian, Marlene Shoemaker.

"No worries," Diana said to Marlene. "I'll bring them home."

She wanted to be the cool parent, different from the stuffy adults who forgot what it was like to be fourteen. If it meant telling a white lie so her little girl could have some happiness, so be it.

What was the worst that could happen?

Diana dropped the girls off and gave them one last warning.

"Get home safe."

It would be the last time she would ever see her daughter again.

THE PHONE CALL

A few hours later, Diana would then receive a phone call from Misty as she tended to her elderly patient. Misty told her that she had missed the bus but could get a ride from Rheuban Schmidt.

Diana, knowing what kind of unsavory character Schmidt was, adamantly refused. She told Misty to find someone else to give her a ride back. Misty had an electronic diary which she used to store phone numbers. She told her mother she would find someone trustworthy to call for a ride.

"You call me back when you find someone," Diana said.

"I will. I promise."

Diana would wait all night for the phone call.

In the ensuing hours, Misty would not call back.

Worried, Diane called home in the hope that Misty had gotten a ride without calling her.

No answer.

Diana didn't panic. She figured that Misty went home with that scumbag Schmidt and didn't want to get yelled out for disobeying her.

She's going to get yelled at either/or. All Diana wanted was for her daughter to be safe.

Her shift finally ended and Diana drove back home in a rush.

Upon entering her house, she called out for Misty.

Silence.

She went into Misty's room and saw that it had been untouched from the previous night.

Diana would call the police in a panic. She told them that her daughter had not come home from the fair. The dispatcher would tell her that the police could not do anything about it for thirty days as it "sounded like a runaway case."

Diana knew otherwise.

Trying to calm herself, she figured that Misty was with Trina, that the two of them would be okay.

She called Trina's home.

No answer.

She then began scorching the earth with phone calls.

She would call Rheuban but he told her that she called but he didn't have the gas to go get her. She then called numerous friends of Misty and her mother.

No one had seen Misty.

She called Trina's home again, got no answer, then drove out to her house. She then went to the police department and filed a formal report with the Pierce County's Sheriff's Department who handled runaways as opposed to the Puyallup Police.

MISTY'S MISSING

Misty's friend Trina called Diana after she came back from school. She told the frantic mother that she didn't know where Misty was.

"The last time I saw her, she was heading for the bus," she said.

Diana would call Rheuban again. She would get his roommate this time, James Tinsley.

Diana needed answers. She interrogated the young fifteen-year-old like a grizzled police detective. She asked if Rheuban had been home all night. James then told her that Rheuban and his uncle went to pick up Misty but that he wasn't home just yet.

Later, Diana would call back and Rheuban would tell her that his roommate got the story wrong. He went to a party instead and didn't pick up Misty. He didn't know where she was.

Diana pleaded for the police to do something. They dragged their heels and began talking to some of Misty's friends. "Just call if she calls," they informed them. "No one gets in trouble."

Diana printed fliers with Misty's picture. She plastered them in and around the fairgrounds while calling the media.

The one woman search team would yield no leads. Rheuban would stop by and ask if the police had found anything yet. Diana would then wait at the bus stop near the fairgrounds to inquire with different drivers on the route. She found one driver who said that he saw Misty. She had asked when the next bus to Spanaway was arriving. The driver said it wasn't and that he was done for the night. He gave her instructions on which bus to take but she walked away before he could complete his sentence.

AN ERROR OF JUDGEMENT

Among the many mistakes that the Puyallup police made in the investigation of Misty's disappearance was to make the assumption that she was a runaway. Why they didn't entertain the prospect that she could have been kidnapped and murdered gave the abductor precious time to cover his tracks.

The police came to this erroneous conclusion after they interviewed Misty's mother, Diana. They thought she was a liar and an alcoholic. They then interviewed a pair of Misty's classmates who really didn't know her that well or accompany her to the fair.

A series of cover-ups then ensued, as the police told the media Misty had been found (where they got that information remains a mystery) and made no further investigation.

Until Diana and the media started to make a fuss. The department had to save face and eventually one of the detectives believed that this was not a runaway case.

Misty's disappearance could not be ignored any longer.

Police would talk to the various fair workers and security guards. No one had recalled seeing Misty.

The police then turned to her family, interviewing and doing background checks on both Misty's father, Buck, and Diana.

Their impressions of the duo would support their initial theory that Misty runaway. Diana was an alcoholic with multiple DUIs and seven years prior she had been convicted of welfare fraud. Buck confirmed that his daughter and Diana would have their issues.

Carver then discovered that Diana had filed a runaway report on Misty a month prior to her disappearing.

Diana would later state that the report was wrong. She thought Misty had disappeared then found her in the bedroom. She was too ashamed to tell the police it had been a false alarm.

With the police questioning and media coverage, Misty Copsey was now the talk of her Spanaway Lake Junior High school.

Rumors would abound at the school, one of which came from Misty Matthews who said that Misty had called her from Olympia. Another student stated that she saw Misty at a Color Me Badd concert at the fair.

The rumors were enough to prompt Carver to remove Misty from the FBI's National Crime Information Center as a missing person. He would once again treat her as a runaway.

BOBER'S THEORY

Cory Bober's knew he was right. He knew that police would find a body of a young woman off Highway 410.

He waited but nothing happened.

Until his mother showed him the flier of Misty's disappearance.

Right again!

Heart racing, he called the number on the flier. Bober would get into contact with Diana and hurriedly told her all about his research.

He talked about the Green River Killer, where and how he killed his victims. He would tell Diana that her disappearance was connected to the same guy responsible for the murdered Puyallup Girls, Kim Delange and Anne Chebetnoy.

Cory would apologize to Diana because he knew that Misty was dead. He predicted her body would be found somewhere along Highway 410.

The two would form an uneasy alliance. Bober became Misty's personal avenger. He would start a phone/letter/media campaign to prove the police wrong and himself right.

Misty was no runaway.

She was a victim of Randall Achziger.

In October, however, Bober would be arrested for selling marijuana. He was then accosted by Sgt.Herm Carver who tired of the young man meddling in police affairs.

"He walked in the room I was being held in – looking tired and pissed off. He said, 'I got out of bed tonight, and came down here to meet you – just to see what kind of a hypocrite you REALLY ARE!'

I said (being cocky), 'It's not MY FAULT – HERM – that you don't believe Misty Copsey's MISSING!!'

He yelled (angry), 'DON'T YOU EVER CALL ME BY MY FIRST NAME – IT'S SGT. CARVER TO YOU!!!'"

Bober's journals, November 1992

THIRTY DAYS MISSING

Sgt. Herm Carver and Deputy Brian Coburn would each individually warn Diana of the troublemaker that Bober was. Still, the worried mother would welcome his assistance as she needed all the help she could get. After numerous phone calls, the two would finally meet after a month of Misty being missing. Diana had nowhere else to turn but to the shaggy-haired twenty-six-year-old who lived with his parents.

The police were going through the motions on their end. Carver reactivated Misty's name on state and national lists but only because he was legally required to do so. At this point, he still believed Misty to be a runaway and doubted Diana's veracity.

Meanwhile, Diana would find Cory Bober's constant badgering to be annoying. It got so bad she filed a restraining order against him.

"My daughter has been missing for six weeks from the Puyallup Fair," Diana wrote in the restraining order. "Cory Bober has called me on a daily basis, telling me my daughter is dead. I was advised by Deputy Brian Coburn to file this complaint if I felt threatened."

The order would only last two weeks. Diana would then call the courts and rescind her request. She would later call Bober and apologize. Her daughter had been missing for over 56 days. Bober was annoying as hell but he was the only one doing research. The only one who cared.

Bober organized a volunteer search for Misty in the Green River area. He somehow coerced someone on the police forensic team to tell him the general vicinity of where one of the Puyallup girl's body was found. Bober surmised that Misty's body would be found in the same general area.

Seventy-two days after Misty had gone missing, there was now a volunteer team searching for her.

Nothing came out of the search.

But Diana would later spot Rheuban at a grocery store and confront him. The young man ran and got into a truck with an older man. She saw the look of fear and apprehension on both men as they sped off.

Diana would then lapse into a depression. She tried to commit suicide with booze and prescription drugs.

The next day she would wake up in a hospital. She would spend the next day there, drying out until being discharged back into the nightmare that had become her life.

A PLEA TO THE PUBLIC

Four months after Misty's disappearance, Diana would appear on a local TV station for a special on the Green River Killer. Jim Doyon, the homicide detective who worked the case, spoke of the killings but deferred on stating if Delange and Chebetnoy(the slain Puyallup girls) were connected.

Doyon took an interest in Misty's case. He would journey to Highway 410 and search near milepost 30 where the bodies of Delange and Chebetnoy had been discovered.

Like Bober and the volunteer search team, he too came up empty.

Bober was undaunted and organized another search. He realized that they had been searching in the wrong spot. They were searching on the south side of the highway when the should have been searching on the north.

Twelve people would show up for the search. Diana would arrive with her older sister, Debra. Bober would arrive with Al Hensley, the father of one of the slain Puyallup girls along with his 14-year old Boy Scout nephew, Jaremy Brown.

It would be the Boy Scout that would make the find

Poking into a ditch with his stick, he saw the crumpled blue jeans. Socks fell out of the jeans.

Baggy and stone-washed, they were cuffed at the bottom. The same jeans that Misty had borrowed from her mother on the night of the fair. The jeans were too big for her and Diana remembered them cuffing them on the bottom.

Bober became excited. He knew that the killer had planted the jeans there as a taunt.

He was right. The police were wrong.

But Diana, according to her sister, "broke into a million pieces."

THE KILLING FIELD

Seven dead women had been found in the nine-mile stretch between Enumclaw and Greenwater in the eight years prior to Misty's disappearance.

The two slain Puyallup girls were found in the same area in 1988 and 1991, only one hundred feet apart. They were left off a footpath that had been hidden by thick brush.

Both of the teenage girls had been presumed abducted from the Puyallup shopping center. Detective Jim Doyon believed privately that the cases were connected. He arrived at the site where Misty's jeans were found and interviewed witnesses, particularly Diana and Bober.

The jeans were taken to the lab and the forensic analysis indicated that the jeans had been in the ditch for some time.

Police suspected that someone (Bober? Diana?) had planted the jeans there.

What was undeniable that the jeans were found only a ten minute walk away from where the bodies of the two slain Puyallup girls were found.

SUSPICIONS ARISE

People began to talk. There were reporters who believed the jeans were planted there. Some were talking as if Diana and Bober were lovers and had plotted this for some insurance money.

Dede Miles, a fifteen-year-old friend of Misty, would come to Sgt. Carver with a tip. She said there was a boy that kept coming over to Misty's parties. He would always leave before her mother came home.

His name was Rheuban Schmidt.

Finally, the unkempt looking young man would come under the radar of the police.

Diana, meanwhile, began to suspect Cory Bober.

How did he know where to look? Why was this stranger so interested in the case to begin with? How did he know so much?

The police had warned her to stay away from him. Now she felt compelled to tell the police of her suspicions.

"Diana comes to station. Now feels Cory Bober may be involved in Misty's disappearance. I asked Diana to submit a written statement to that effect and why she feels he may be involved – she agreed to do so."

Carver's notes

AN INTERVIEW WITH TRINA

Detective Jim Doyon would interview the fifteen-year-old Trina Bevard, the last person to see Misty alive.

Six months had passed. Doyon had brought along the jeans with him, the sight of which made Trina cry.

"It seems to me like something that Misty was wearing that night," Trina said. "It looks very close to what Misty was wearing. The socks, they match what she was wearing. The jeans are big, so – her jeans were baggy that night, that she was wearing. They're – they were light blue like they are in the photo. It just seems, you know, it was the clothes that she was wearing."

Doyon would go on to ask what she was wearing (a pullover) and if she had any jewelry. He then asked if she had any cigarettes or birth control pills.

"No," Trina said. "She was straight. She was a virgin. She didn't smoke, she didn't drink, she didn't do drugs. She was clean, so she had no reason to do anything. She wasn't sexually active."

Trina then revealed that the girls made five calls to Rheuban. They could not get a hold of him. They finally got him on the line and he still refused to pick them up even when the girls offered him money. Misty told him about a key under the front doormat of her home. He could go inside, get money for gas and come pick them up.

Trina stated that she didn't trust Rheuban but only because he didn't keep his word and come pick them up. She then called a 23-year old friend named Mike Rhyner for a ride but they got disconnected. The girls were then stranded. They walked downtown to get to the bus stop before spotting a phone booth by a convenience store. Misty then called her mother, telling her that if Rheuban didn't come pick her up she would take the bus. The two argued as Diana didn't want Misty around Rheuban.

Trina had to get home by 10 p.m. She had about an hour and a half to get home which wasn't that far. Misty could not walk the ten miles to Spanaway.

Trina then decided to walk. She gave Misty her extra money for the bus.

"At that time I made my decision of walking home and she said she would take the bus," Trina recalled. "The last words that I said to her were 'Be careful,' and she turned around and told me the same and we walked off in different directions"

Trina also dismissed the notion of Misty being a runaway.

" Her mom just bought her a stereo and she was so excited and she went shopping and she got new clothes," Trina recalled. She was telling me all about it. She was really excited about it.

BOBER GOES TO JAIL

Meanwhile, Bober would be sentenced to fourteen months in prison for the marijuana possession. He felt that the sentencing was too punitive and threatened law enforcement that they would never find Misty without him. His fellow inmates thought he was crazy and began calling him "snitch" and "The Green River Killer".

Jail would not slow down Bober's efforts, however. He continued to research and write Misty's mother.

"Dear Diana,

...When we found Misty's clothes, part of me died and I watched a part of you die too (much more than a "part") and I was at a total loss for words. I never wanted to be the one to show you your most horrible fears were true and that your daughter is truly dead at the hands of a sick murderer. I will never rest until the killer (Randy Achziger) is brought to justice and dead, if it takes my life to do it."

AMERICA'S MOST WANTED

Misty's case would eventually be broadcast nationally as it was featured on the America's Most Wanted television show.

Over twenty-eight tips came into Sgt. Carver from people who watched the broadcast.

When the tips went nowhere, Diana's suspicions returned to her original suspect, Rheuban Schmidt. She wanted Carver to speak to the young man but the Sergeant would take a circuitous route to get to Schmidt.

Carver would speak to Frank Rodriguez, the owner of Adam's Ribs, a restaurant where Rheuban worked. He convinced the owner to try and find out how much Rheuban knew about Misty.

"3-4-93 @ 1500: Frank states Rheuban said the following during a lengthy conversation about Misty Copsey:

- Yeah, I know about it.

- I know exactly where she is buried.

- They found the clothes but she is buried 6 miles from there.

- They're off by 6 or 6 1/2 miles."

— Excerpt from Carver's notes

Carver would then wait for Rheuban outside the restaurant before his shift started. Schmidt arrived, saw the cops and immediately ran off. The detectives would eventually catch up with him.

Rheuban would concede that he had received calls from Misty the night of her disappearance. But his story corroborated with Trina's, he told the girls he had no gas and could not pick them up.

Carver then asked if he knew where Misty was buried but Rheuban was adamant that he "said those things to get Frank off my back."

Rheuban then revealed that he suffered from "black outs". He stated that he did not recall anything until the daylight hours of September 18th, 1992.

The detectives pounced, asking if it was possible that he blacked out, picked up Misty and harmed her.

Rheuban claimed he didn't know.

All he knew was that he drove out to his grandmother's farmhouse and couldn't recall why.

Detectives would then give Rheuban a polygraph test.

They would later state that the suspect "zoned out" during the test, nearly falling asleep. The tests were inconclusive but detectives felt as if he were trying to beat the test.

A LITTLE LIE

Rheuban fell off the detective's radar when Carver talked to Dede Miles again. Dede would tell the detective that Trina had not walked home from the fairground like she told him.

Dede said that Trina had a boyfriend come pick her up and didn't want anyone to know.

Trina's boyfriend's name was Michael J. Rhyner. He had nothing on his record aside from traffic stops but he had friends that were connected with Chebetnoy and Delange.

He also had a complaint when he was sixteen years old. He was accused of an abduction rape wherein he used a knife and a cigarette lighter to terrorize an eleven-year-old.

Charges were never filed for an undisclosed reason.

Carver brought Trina in for more questioning. He wanted the truth. The truth about who picked her up that night. The truth about Misty.

But the truth was that Trina told the Sgt. Carver and Detective Tom Matison that she lied because she feared "getting into trouble with her guardian about it."

Trina admitted that she called Rhyner, got disconnected and left a message. She told Misty that they could both ride with Rhyner but Misty said no.

"Trina would not be specific why Misty did not trust Rhyner, but the indication was that Rhyner might have 'come on' to Misty at one time and she did not like it. Trina states that she and Rhyner are friends, but not involved."

— Matison's notes

Trina said that she started to walk and then Rhyner picked her up and dropped her off. The detectives asked if perhaps Rhyner had picked up Misty but she said no.

FRANK RODRIGUEZ' FOLLOW UP

Diana would state that Frank Rodriguez, Rheuban's employer, would call her to say that Rheuban had "bragged about doing something" to Misty with his uncle. Frank didn't fully believe him, however, as Rheuban was "weird" and always bragging about stuff he didn't do.

Diana then approached Carver about Rheuban and the sergeant went ballistic.

"We have our man!" he said.

The man he sought was Michael Rhyner, Trina Bevard's boyfriend.

"We share our knowledge of Mike Rhyner and how he is involved with Misty and Trina – and the fact Trina lied to Doyon. We state that there is an excellent possibility that Rhyner may be linked to Chebetnoy and DeLange. Exchange of information is extremely beneficial."

— Carver's notes

"Sgt. Carver believes that Rhyner dropped Bevard off, returned to the area of the fairgrounds, located Misty Copsey, convinced her to get into his vehicle and drove off with her."

— Doyon's notes

Police set up a sting on Rhyner. The car mechanic was selling his 1981 blue Ford Escort for $200 bucks.

The buyer was an undercover cop.

He watched as Rhyner hurriedly took out trash from the car before the sale. The police then did a forensic examination of the car.

Meanwhile, Rheuban's green Nova was being crushed at a wrecking yard. The Puyallup police didn't care as the tweaker was no longer on their radar. Also, Randy Achziger, Bober's suspect, had been charged and convicted for the rape of a seven-year-old.

INTERROGATING RHYNER

Ideally, Detectives Matison and Sgt. Carver wanted the forensics back from Rhyner's Escort before they spoke to him. But the wait became interminable and they brought him in for questioning without some evidence to back up their suspicions.

Rhyner's story would match that of Trina's. He picked Trina up and went back home. He said that he and Trina were only "good friends" and he had met Misty only four times. Matison then asked Rhyner if he felt Misty was alive and what should happen to the person who harmed her.

Rhyner knew what the detective was getting at. On his own volition, Rhyner told the detectives about his juvenile complaint from years ago. He stated he had been cleared and knew that was why they were looking at him now.

"First thing I thought, you know, well, that's in my file," Rhyner said. "Now you guys are going to think I did it since it's in my file. About Misty, that's the one thing that worried me."

Rhyner then passed a polygraph test.

Grasping at straws, the police then turned their sights back on Rheuban. If only they had impounded his car when they had the chance...

TOO LITTLE TOO LATE

"Rheuban Schmidt's initial interview with Sgt. Carver and I created more questions than answers. He was very vague about what he did that September 17th and finally said that he had a 'blackout' and 'woke up' at his grandmother's property near Enumclaw.

...Schmidt had told Frank Rodriguez that Misty's body was six miles from where the jeans were found. He now claims that he said this just to get Rodriguez "off his back," and was not a true statement.

He was driving a Green Chev Nova at the time but he no longer has the vehicle. It was repossessed.

Schmidt also mentioned that his Grandmother's property is located in King County by Buckley and is over a hundred acres. The property has cows on it. Few people enter onto the property."

— Matison's notes

Tinsley, fifteen years old at the time of Misty's disappearance, told police the Rheuban was his roommate for only a few months. He described Rheuban as a short-tempered guy who had a thirteen-year-old girlfriend. The girlfriend, Tinsley said, got jealous when Rheuban got a call from Misty.

Tinsley stated that Rheuban had left the apartment in a huff then came back between eleven and one at night.

So Rheuban did not "black out" as he told detectives. N

"What do you think might have happened to her?" Matison asked.

"Um, I couldn't, I couldn't say because I have no idea," Tinsley said.

"Well, can you speculate?"

"With Rheuban, this is just that I, this, this is what I say with Rheuban because I, I figure that um that he, he tried to, he tried to um, get with her or something and she said, she said no and he got all pissed and did something, I don't know, that's just a second guess."

"You think Rheuban would be capable of ah, kidnapping and killing somebody?"

"I think he could," Tinsley said.

Detectives would meet with Rheuban again, relaying the information that Tinsley recalled him coming back to the apartment that night.

But Rheuban remained adamant in stating that he didn't remember what he did. The detectives then drove him out to his grandmother's farm which had over 100-acres...100 secluded acres.

Detective Matison would note that Rheuban's grandmother's house six miles north of Buckley. Rheuban told Frank that Misty would be buried six miles away from where her jeans were found which would place it in the close vicinity of his grandmother's farm. They would go to inquire with his grandmother but she was not home.

They did not follow-up with the grandmother .

Even so, Rheuban's story no longer held up. He told Misty that he didn't have any gas. He lived sixteen miles away from the fair.

But then he stated that he had driven to his grandmother's farm in Buckley then returned home.

A sixty-mile round trip.

Detectives would give him another polygraph test which he passed.

"It appears that Rheuban Schmidt was not involved in the disappearance of Misty Copsey. He, however, has no alibi as to his movements during the evening of her disappearance, as well as no memory; he claimed that he had a blackout. He acknowledges that he left the residence of James Tinsley, but does not remember what he did.

Investigation to continue."

— Matison's notes

ONE YEAR ANNIVERSARY

The local media ran a few more stories on Misty's disappearance as the Puyallup Fair started. The forensic test on Rhyner's test finally came through. There was no match

with Misty anywhere.

Now once again grasping at straws, Carver would turn to Diana and her associates. He would interview Diana's parole officer and one of her ex-boyfriends.

Misty's father, Buck, was asked to take a polygraph test. He gave consent and passed.

"I explained to her that missing person investigations, at some point in time, must eliminate the parents of any wrongdoing. Diana agreed to the examination."

— Carver's notes

Diana would pass her polygraph test but Jim Corey, Doyon's colleague, said that Diana's polygraph would prove to be inconclusive and that perhaps she had something to do with planting the jeans at the location on Hwy 410.

Carver had always had his doubts about Diana and felt that she planted the jeans.

But the leads would eventually dry up. After nine years, Misty Copsey's disappearance would turn cold.

No one was ever charged with her disappearance.

THE AFTERMATH

Diana would hand out fliers at the Puyallup Fairgrounds every year. She was doing more than law enforcement and even the media.

Every now and then, a local reporter would run a story about Misty. A few cranks would call in and say that they knew something but it would lead to nowhere. Then that would be it. Everything would run dry.

Detective Jim Doyon felt that she was deceased.

BOBER TO THE RESCUE

Bober was then caught for marijuana possession again but this time, he pressed for an advantage. He would gain the Washington State Patrol crime lab report on Misty's jeans, compiled after their 1993 discovery.

He argued that the lab report was part of his defense....he gambled and won.

Obtaining the prized document, the amateur sleuth went to work. The report stated there was no blood, no semen. But there were hairs, fibers, and three red paint chips. There were also holes in the left leg in the jeans, above the knee.

Bober knew that somehow, someway, Randy Achziger was involved. That he killed Misty.

The forensic details raced through Bober's head...red paint chips...red paint chips...

He knew that Bober had a red Porsche. He knew that the paint chips would match.

But the police had another suspect they didn't tell anyone about.

Robert Leslie Hickey.

Hickey's hunting ground was the Puyallup area where he specialized in abduction rapes.

He also drove a red Camaro.

Puyallup police had him on their list as a possible suspect but he was never questioned nor did they obtain forensic samples from his car.

Thirteen years later, however, they would collect samples from Achziger's old car. The car had been sold and the new owner was open to having forensics performed on it.

The particles would be sent to a crime lab which already had a backlog of over a year.

With nothing else left to do, the police turned once again to Rheuban Schmidt.

"I think it's worth taking another shot at Schmidt, and we're planning on it. He's been clean since 1993 ...

— Excerpt from notes by Lt. Dave McDonald, March 19, 2006

Only Schmidt had not been clean. He had been convicted of second-degree theft in 2000. In early 1996, he was accused of rape by one of Misty's best friends. He had held a pillow over her face to silence her but two weeks after filing the report, the girl back away from her accusation and did not file charges.

"[She] told me that she would be undergoing counseling related to the rape, but that she did not want to undergo any additional stress that may be caused by further investigation or possible prosecution in this matter.

Case cleared exceptional/refused by victim."

— Pierce County sheriff's report, Feb. 6, 1996

Later in 2006, Puyallup police gathered more reports on Rheuban. One was a domestic violence protection order requested by his wife, the mother of his three children.

"Rheuban has previously told her that if she ever had him served with a court order he'd 1) burn her house down with her and her kids in it, and 2) send 'some guys' to kick in her door and take money from her.

(She) said Rheuban told her that they'd get money from her if they had to beat her, rape her and then rob her.

(She) said Rheuban told her that if it came to that she 'wouldn't be breathing' when they were done with her."

— Pierce County Sheriff's report, Nov. 9, 2006

MISSING PAINT CHIPS

Adding more incompetence to the investigation, the red paint chips found on Misty's jeans would turn up "missing." All that remained inside the bag where the chips were marked was a piece of plastic.

The lab technicians now had no way to match the red chips on Misty's jeans to Achziger's red Porsche.

Bober would claim that the red chips did match and the police were now trying to save face. Diana, however, no longer wants anything to do with him.

Bober would state that the police would tell Diana that they had, in fact, tested the red paint found on Misty's clothes against Achziger's Porsche. Bober discovered that the red paint was missing beforehand yet the police would lie to Diana about the test.

The lies and incompetence that began investigation have seemingly ended it as well. The Puyallup police relied far too heavily on polygraph tests to discount suspects where their own accounts (particularly in the case of Schmidt) were shaky at best. They failed to secure possession of Schmidt's Green Nova which may have proven to provide forensic evidence that Misty was in his vehicle.

Twenty-four years have elapsed since Misty's disappearance.

Her case remains unsolved.

THE RAILROAD KILLER

They called him the 'Railroad Killer.'

Angel Resendiz earned the nickname because of his penchant for committing his crimes near railroads, using the rail cars as his own personal get-away system.

Committing murder after murder, he was able to elude both American and Mexican authorities for over a decade.

EARLY LIFE

A birth certificate found by the FBI listed his date of birth as August 1st, 1960. He was born To Virginia de Maturino in the town of Izucar de Matomoros in the state of Puebla, Mexico. His mother has stated adamantly that the correct spelling of his surname is Recendis not Resendiz although the killer would have over fifty different aliases throughout his lifetime.

Angel had spent his childhood years with relatives and not with his immediate family. According to his mother, he was sexually abused by an uncle and other pedophiles in the town of Puebla. He would spend his youth roaming the streets, robbing, stealing and sniffing glue. Relatives would later testify that Resendiz was routinely beaten as a child, one time being "jumped" by several other youths who beat him so bad that he bled through his ears. Resendiz would leave home for months at a time then suddenly return mumbling about a coming religious apocalypse.

Legal trouble came early for Resendiz as he was caught trying to sneak into the Texas border at the age of sixteen. This would become the first of numerous run-ins with border patrol agents until he finally made it into the United States, making his way to St. Louis and finding work with a manufacturing company under an assumed name. He even registered to vote with his false identification.

In September of 1979, at the age of nineteen, Resendiz was arrested for assault and car theft in Miami. He was tried and sentenced to twenty-years in prison but was released after only six years and sent back to Mexico.

But he wouldn't stay there for long.

Through numerous attempts of trial and error, Resendiz had learned not only to game the system but to enter and exit the United States with minimal detection.

He learn to use the rail-cars...

AN "INVISIBLE" MAN

Resendiz became so skilled at crossing the border without detection that he began charging for his services. He began to make a living as a human smuggler, transporting Mexicans across the border for a fee.

Resendiz soon developed a reputation for his smuggling skills, often being seen as a 'go to' person in his Ciudad Juarez neighborhood called 'Patria.'

He would make weekly crossings over the border, being arrested only intermittently. He would then be deported back into his native land only to ping-pong back and forth.

Finally, Resendiz would serve prison terms for his crimes. He would be arrested in Texas for false identity and citizenship, getting a year and half worth of jail.

Upon release in 1987, he journeyed to New Orleans and was arrested for carrying a concealed weapon. He received another year and half worth of prison time until parole.

He then went back to his old haunts in St. Louis where he tried to defraud Social Security and receive illegal payments. He got caught and served a three year sentence.

Resendiz then decided small-time burglaries were his deal. He once again illegally crossed the border, journeyed to New Mexico and was caught burglarizing a home. He was imprisoned for eighteen months and upon release he broke into a Santa Fe rail yard, being captured yet again.

"They should have called Resendiz the boomerang man," forensic psychologist Frank Lizzo said. "He knew how to play the game and seemingly had no fear of the system. The system never punished him severely enough for him to stop his crimes, let alone stop crossing the border."

After his last recorded deportation, the killings began.

THE KILLING FIELDS

"He probably started killing somewhere in his late 20s," Douglas said. "He may have killed people like himself initially – males, transients...(he) became angry at the population at large. What America represents here is this wealthy country where he keeps getting kicked out...(he) just can't make ends meet. Coupled with these feelings, these inadequacies, fueled by the fact that he's known to take alcohol, take drugs, lowers his inhibitions now to go out and kill."

Angel's list of victims began in 1986. Continuing to bounce in and out of the United States, he shot a homeless woman and left her for dead in an abandoned farm house. He had met the acquaintance of the woman at a homeless shelter and they became friends. They would later take a trip on a motorcycle together when he felt that the woman disrespected him.

Resendiz would then take out his gun and blow her head off.

The woman allegedly had a boyfriend whom Resendiz shot and killed as well. He said that he dumped his body in a creek between San Antonio and Uvalde. This killing has never been verified aside from what Resendiz revealed to the police during his interrogation sessions.

Five years later, Resendiz would kill Michael White because he was a "homosexual." Resendiz would bludgeon White to death with a brick and leave him in front of an abandoned home.

These were seemingly warm-ups for the more brutal crimes to come which would also include rape.

"Sex seemed almost secondary," FBI profiler John Douglas said when apprised of Resendiz's crimes. "(He is) just a bungling crook ...very disorganized."

Douglas would later concede, however, that it was this disorganization that worked in his favor. Like a true drifter, Resendiz' whereabouts became as elusive as a rational thought in his head.

"When he hitches a ride on the freight train, he doesn't necessarily know where the train is going," Douglas said. "But when he gets off, having background as a burglar, he's able to scope out the area, do a little surveillance, make sure he breaks into the right house where there won't be anyone to give him a run for his money. He can enter a home complete with cutting glass and reaching in and undoing the locks."

"He'll look through the windows and see who's occupying it. The guy's only 5 foot-7, very small. In fact...the early weapons were primarily blunt-force trauma weapons, weapons of opportunity found at the scenes. He has to case them out, make sure he can put himself in a win-win situation."

Resendiz would also leave his weapon of choice up to chance. Whatever the home would have, a statue a mantle piece, a butcher knife, that would become the instrument of murder.

FLORIDA KILLINGS

On March 23rd, 1997, Jesse Howell would be found bludgeoned to death beside the railroad tracks in Ocala, Florida. He was nineteen years old.

"When we got there," Sheriff Patty Lumpkin said. "We see what appears to be a young male, in his late teens or early twenties. Blood around the head area. You could tell by looking at him that he was dead. The first thing I do is make sure that we've got our forensics people on the way, on the medical examiners on the way, and all the investigators that we have called out or either there or en route."

"When those types of things happen it might have been someone who had fallen off a train," Lt. Jeff Owens said. "Or someone who could have been struck by a train."

The authorities quickly ruled out an accident, however, as they examined the body.

"It didn't appear to be an accident," Lumpkin said. "Because if he had been hit by the train the trauma would have been much more extreme. I've seen some deaths from trains and the initial impact from the train would have done more harm to the body."

The forensic team did determine that Howell's body looked as if he were the victim of blunt force trauma.

"We did see a baseball type of cap," forensic scientist Michael Dunn said. "It appeared to have blood on the inside surface of he bill. In addition, there was a pair of wire rimmed eye glasses and one of the eye pieces was missing, one of the lenses was out. This didn't look good either. As we moved closer, we saw that the victim had been dragged to that spot using just the blue jean material around the cuff (of his pants)."

Near the body, they found a brass and rubber coupling. This device was used to link one train car to another. It could also be used as a clubbing weapon.

"It had what appeared to be blood on it (the coupling)," Dunn recalled.

Howell still had jewelry on his person. He wore a gold cross necklace, a watch and a small amount of cash in his pocket. The police ruled out robbery as a motive.

The police did not identify Howell's body right off the bat. They did find a money wire receipt where some money had been wired from Illinois to Florida. The name on the receipt was of a woman named "Wendy."

Police tracked the money transfer to its point of origin which was all the way in Woodstock, Illinois.

Coincidentally, the authorities there were investigating the disappearance of Wendy Von Huben.

Wendy was missing alongside her boyfriend, the nineteen year old Jesse Howell.

"They advised me that they were investigating a John Doe," Woodstock Detective Kurt Rosenquest recalled. "Unidentified male."

Rosenquest then followed up with the investigating team in Florida, sending them the fingerprints and pictures of Jesse Howell.

The Ocala police would then positively identify Howell.

Jesse had met Wendy only months earlier. They had secretly planned to marry and went on a road trip with another couple.

The other couple, however, grew tired of Jesse and Wendy's constant bickering. They demanded to be let out of the car and left. Jesse and Wendy continued into Ocala, Florida where they ran out of money.

Wendy would call her parents in Illinois who would then transfer her $200 via Western Union. The couple would collect the $200 but would not return home.

"We checked Greyhounds," Rosenquest said. "Nobody matching their description ordered buses or train tickets back to the Woodstock area."

Tears were shed as Rosenquest informed Howell's parents that their teen son had been murdered. The investigative team then turned their attention to the disappearance of Wendy.

They held out hope because there were issues between her and Jesse, thinking that perhaps she simply ran off to be by herself.

Police scoured the surrounding areas and used helicopters in all directions around the railroad tracks.

They would find nothing. There was no DNA left behind on Jesse Howell's body either.

Papers and fliers with Wendy Von Huben's information was distributed all throughout Florida up through Illinois.

Authorities also began interviewing the transient population that lived along the railroad tracks.

Two and a half months later, however, Wendy's parents would receive a phone call.

"The phone rang," Rosenquest recalled. "Wendy's father answered the phone. The girl was crying. She said 'I'm sorry. I love you.'"

She would tell the father she was two hours away from Woodstock at a gas station. The father asked for the phone number on the pay phone she was calling from and she said that there wasn't any before hanging up.

The police were not certain that the phone call came from Wendy so they immediately headed out to the gas station where they believe the call took place.

Police tracked down the surveillance video of the gas station. On the video, a woman that physically resembled Wendy entered the gas station.

The phone records, however, revealed that the call did not come from the gas station where the surveillance video revealed a woman who allegedly was Wendy. It came from another gas station where there were fliers posted of Wendy.

Someone had played a cruel hoax as Wendy's parents had added their home number to the fliers

ONE-LEGGED BOB AND A CHANCE DISCOVERY

A year went by without any sign of Wendy.

There was some ray of hope, however, as the railroad authorities called the Ocala police and informed them that the received information from a member of one of the homeless camps. They had a man in custody named "One Legged Bob" who was traveling with a girl and may be responsible for the murder of her previous boyfriend.

"'One Legged Bob' was your typical homeless person," Owens said. "Kinda scruffy. Hadn't shaved in a few days. He had a prosthetic leg that helped him get around. For someone who you might consider crippled, he was far from crippled."

Owens would spend the next eight hours interviewing the only lead he had, a one legged homeless man.

After the grueling interrogation, Owens realized that he had the wrong suspect.

By sheer chance, however, Patty Lumpkin heard about someone they dubbed the "Railroad Killer" during a class she was taking at the FBI.

"They called him the Railway Killer," Lumpkin recalled. "The Angel of Death. He was killing people. Leaving them near the railroad or he was killing them at homes or locations that were close to the railroad.

The FBI knew the Railway Killer as Angel Resendiz.

"We knew that Angel Resendiz was a person that rode the rails across the country," FBI Agent Mark Young said. "We were worried where he'd wind up next. So we decided to make him a top ten fugitive. Maybe the millions of eyes of the public would tell us something."

The strategy worked.

"He was one of the most vile, evil persons that I had ever dealt with," Young said. "It was like every time you turn around there's another murder."

Owens and Lumpkin hoped to talk to Resendiz to query him about Jesse Howell's murder and Wendy Von Huben's disappearance.

"The attorneys representing him at the time in Texas stopped us," Owens said. "They wanted to protect their client from talking. Any defense attorney who represents a criminal will generally tell the person to stop talking to law enforcement."

Resendiz was placed on death row and Texas had a fast execution rate. The two detectives worried that they would lose their chance to interview Resendiz and connect him to the crimes in Ocala.

Owens and Lumpkin decided to mail Resendiz a letter, respectfully asking him if they could interview him. The letter was written in a formal manner and even addressed him as "Senor."

To their surprise, Resendiz responded back and granted them an interview regarding his involvement in Jesse's killing and Wendy's disappearance.

During their meeting, Resendiz was quick to admit that he had killed Jesse. The detectives deliberately withheld information about the killing, holding back details that only the killer would know. But when Resendiz described using a brake coupling from one of the trains, they knew they had their killer.

But they needed to find out what happened to Wendy.

In a follow-up letter, they promised him immunity from prosecution if he agreed to talk. It was a moot point by then as he was already on death row but the detectives still needed permission from Wendy's family to go through with the interview.

In order to receive some sense of closure, the family agreed to the immunity.

"When we get to the prison," Lumpkin said. "We see him coming down the hallway. He (Resendiz) has a waist belt on. It's an electric shock belt and he's chained to the belt. He's just a mild-mannered person but remember that a psychopath or a sociopath doesn't have any feeling. I mean he had dead eyes. He had no feeling in that body. He didn't care about anything."

Resendiz would reveal that he was heading south for work when the train stopped and he spotted Jesse getting off the train for a smoke.

"Resendiz told us that he killed Jesse with a piece of the train coupling," Lumpkin said. "And Wendy was asleep on the train when this took place. And then when they went down the road further somehow he talked Wendy into getting off the train."

Resendiz then raped and strangled Wendy to death.

Resendiz drew a map of where had left Wendy's body. He described burying her in a shallow grave near a canopy of trees. Resendiz would remember that she had a book in a back pack and an army style jacket that he used to cover her fresh grave.

Police would return to the site and were able to locate where he buried Wendy's body. Almost three years after the murder, everything the killer described was still there. The book. The jacket.

And Wendy's body.

"When Wendy ran away she had a small engagement ring," Owen said. "And she had a Winnie the Pooh wristwatch.

The detective would bring those items back to Wendy's parents.

KENTUCKY RAILROAD MURDER

In August of 1997, Resendiz would make his way from Ocala, Florida to Lexington, Kentucky. It was there he would stalk two young college students.

Holly Dunn was a 20-year old junior at the University of Kentucky and it was there she met Christopher Maier.

"Chris Maier was my very good friend," Dunn recalled. "He was just the nicest, kindest man. We decided that we wanted to be more than friends then we started dating. We dated for about three months."

"Chris and I were attending a party. We decided that the party wasn't very fun so we went to go talk a walk by the railroad tracks. We sat down and talked for awhile and when we got up to leave a man came out from behind an electrical box. He had a weapon that he used on Chris. It was some sort of ice pick or screw driver. Something sharp. I guess our immediate thought was he's going to rob us. That's when we realize he wants money we start thinking 'okay, well, you could have our credit card, you can have our ATM card, you can have our car.' Then he started tying up Chris' hands behind his back. And then he came over to me and he took off my belt and that's when I started thinking he doesn't want to rob us."

After tying up Holly, Resendiz then pulled Chris by the shirt across the railroad tracks and into a ditch.

Holly would follow on her knees, pleading for him to stop whatever he was about to do.

"Lie down," Resendiz said, his voice soft but menacing.

"Everything is going to be okay," Christopher said to Holly as Resendiz dragged him into the ditch.

"Shut up!" Resendiz commanded as he gagged Christopher with a sock.

Resendiz then walked off into the darkness. The frightened couple did not know what the psychopath had planned.

"Then he comes with this rock," Holly recalled. "There was no warning, he drops this rock on Chris' head. I'm just thinking 'what just happened?' I don't even know what just happened."

"You don't have to worry about him anymore," Resendiz said to Holly as he got on top of her.

"I went into survival mode, I'm thinking, I mean he's gonna kill me. I may as well fight. I'm gonna fight. He unties my feet and climbs on top of me. I start to kick and scream and hit him but he held that knife or ice pick (to my throat) and said 'look how easily I could kill you.' I stopped everything and then he raped me."

"I memorized his face," Dunn said. "I stared at him and memorized, he had a tattoo on his arm, I was thinking if you have any scars I'm gonna remember your scars, I'm gonna remember your face,I'm not gonna forget it because if I live through this I will get you."

Resendiz completed the sexual assault of Dunn before smashing her head with a rock.

"He hit me five or six times in my face," Dunn recalled. "I think I put my hand up and then I turned over and then he hit me five or six times in the back of my head. He hit me hard. He was trying to kill me. I think I laid there and he thought I was dead."

Resendiz did think she was did as he threw the rock down and ran away from the crime scene.

Holly would suffer severe facial trauma but miraculously survived the attack.

"I had a broken jaw," Dunn said. "Broken eye socket and cuts on the back of my head that they had to staple shut and then I had cuts on my face."

She woke up in a Kentucky hospital, surrounded by family members.

"Everyone was told not to talk about Chris to me. I just said 'Chris is dead, isn't he?' And my Dad actually is the one I said that to and he was like 'yes, he died.'"

TEXAS TERROR

Resendiz would travel to Texas via train and in October of 1988 he flopped down in Hughes Springs. He would enter the home of 87-year old Leafie Mason, attacking the woman with an iron and killing her.

Two months later, Resendiz would sneak into the home of Dr. Claudia Benton, a thirty-nine year old medical researcher who lived in a suburb of Houston near the railroad tracks.

Again, it was a case of a home being to close to the train tracks. The train would provide the perfect cover for the sneaky Resendiz as he realized that the sound of the rail-car racing by would allow him to break in homes without being heard.

He applied the same technique with Benton, breaking into her home, raping then killing her.

Police would find the doctor face down on the floor. Her bedroom soaked in blood, ransacked for any valuables.

He head had been covered in a plastic bag while her body had been covered in a blanket.

"It appears that she (Claudia Benton) was sleeping," recalled Ken Macha, former police sergeant. "He was able to get in and picked up a bronze statuette from the mantle in the living room. He was relentless in beating her. The skull fractures themselves would have been enough to kill her. She was then stabbed in the back with a very large butcher knife."

"Resendiz was brutal, sadistic," said former West University police chief Gary Brye.

Fingerprints and DNA evidence would link Resendiz to the crime.

The problem was they could catch the man that Texas Ranger Drew Carter referred to as "a walking, breathing form of evil."

EVADING POLICE

Seven months later, Resendiz would continue to avoid capture. He remained in Texas, riding the rail cars until coming into the town of Weimar. He would break into the home of Pastor Norman "Skip" Sirnic and his wife Karen. Resendiz smashed a jack hammer into both of their heads, killing them instantly. He would then rape the body of Karen postmortem.

"He would watch these places," prosecuting attorney Devin Anderson said. "He would watch them, wait for them to go to sleep, get in their house and he would strike them before they would even wake up. I thought we have got to catch this guy."

The DNA found at the scene of the Sirnic murders would match those left on Benton. The FBI then realized they had a highly mobile serial killer on the loose...someone who could kill in one town then appear in another town miles away and kill again.

Resendiz was also smart. He would constantly alter his appearance. He'd shave his head. Then his mustache. He'd be clean shaven one week. Unkempt the next. He would wear glasses one week. No glasses the next.

Authorities could not get an accurate description of him other than the fact that he was small.

Resendiz was also able to take advantage of the lack of a coordinated computer system that gave law enforcement the ability to cross-check fugitives. After the Sirnic murders, Border Patrol had encountered Resendiz near the El Paso border but did not find him on the wanted list.

They then deported him back to Mexico.

Within 48 hours, Resendiz was back across the border to resume his killing spree.

"Our computers told us that he was nothing of lookout material," said C.G. Almengor, a supervisor at the border."We really wish he had been in the system so we could have caught him."

Resendiz would be deported no less than seventeen times over the course of his rampage. At no point did authorities make the connection because of his changing appearance, use of different aliases and the lack of a connected system to document illegals trying to come across the border.

A PREFERENCE FOR TEXAS

Noemi Dominguez was a graduate of Rice University who had just recently quit her job as an elementary school teacher to pursue a master's degree.

She was described as "the sweetest, nicest teacher – a darling who went the extra mile."

Fueled by hate, Resendiz would break into Noemi's home and rape her before killing her with a pick ax. He then stole her car and drove to Schulenberg, Texas where he would kill Josephine Konvicka with the same pick ax.

He would leave the weapon embedded in Konvicka's head as well as leave his fingerprints all over the home. He was more than just sloppy, he was getting cocky. He left a newspaper article that described his crimes as well as a toy train...a reference to his nickname as the "Railroad Killer."

Resendiz was also meticulous in approaching his victims.

"He undid the light in her (Noemi's) car," Anderson said. "So when he opened the door it wouldn't come on. That's who were were dealing with. Someone who really knew how to sneak around. Who really knew how to avoid detection."

"He kept killing people. He would not stop. In his mode of transportation, using the railroads was brilliant because they couldn't be monitored. I mean there's thousands of trains and millions of miles of tracks all over the United States."

"I felt hopeless at the time. Because if you're willing to sleep in a train or you're willing to sleep in a field, you can stay lost for a long, long time and I didn't think we were ever going to catch him."

Later that month, Resendiz had journeyed to Illinois, reaching the town of Gorham. He would break into the home of 80-year old George Morber and his daughter Carolyn Frederick. Resendiz would tie Morber to a chair and shoot him in the back of the head with a shotgun. He then raped Carolyn and smashed the shotgun across her head with such force that the weapon broke in half.

Both Morber and Frederick would die from their injuries.

The FBI placed him on their Top Ten list.

They then recruited his common-law wife, Julietta Reyes, and brought her into Houston for questioning from her hometown of Rodeo, Mexico.

Reyes complied with police requests, turning over over ninety-three pieces of jewelry that her husband had mailed to her from the U.S.

Relatives of Noemi Dominguez claimed thirteen pieces. George Benton was able to identify some pieces of jewelry as belonging to his wife as well.

Police would then locate Resendiz's half-sister, Manuela Karkiewicz, who lived in New Mexico. Initially, she refused to cooperate. She worried that the FBI or the police would kill her brother. But Carter convinced her to talk Resendiz into giving himself up.

The FBI knew that Resendiz had made his way back to Mexico after the murders in Illinois and was hiding in his hometown neighborhood of Patria.

Carter was able to get a rapport with Manuela. He convinced her that Resendiz would receive "personal safety while in jail, regular visiting rights for his family and a psychological evaluation."

"I came away with the impression that they (Resendiz' family) definitely had an understanding of right and wrong ... and knew now that what Maturino Resendiz was accused of doing was heinous and wrong ... ," Carter said. "Manuela, especially, came across as a woman of strong faith. There was a very deep emotional strain and burden placed on her in this investigation. She had to make some very difficult choices that impacted her and her family. And, in the end, her actions alone speak to her character."

Carter spent weeks talking to Manuela who in turn "worked a miracle."

They got the serial killer to surrender.

On July 12th, Manuela would receive a fax from the district attorney's office in Harris County which formalized everything that Texas Ranger Carter had promised.

The word passed from Manuela to another relative who acted as a go-between with Resendiz. The relative than came back later that evening and said that Resendiz would surrender in the morning at 9 a.m.

Texas Ranger Drew Carter would accompany Manuela and a spiritual adviser to meet with Resendiz on a bridge that connected El Paso, Texas to Ciudad Juarez.

"When I saw that face there was a little bit of excitement there because I finally said, 'This is going to happen,'" Carter recalled as he remembered Resendiz appearing on the bridge with his dirty jeans, muddy boots and blank facial expression. "He stuck out his hand, I stuck out my hand, and we shook hands."

Resendiz would then surrender to the Texas Ranger.

DEATH PENALTY

Resendiz' attorneys knew that their only hope would be an insanity defense. The Mexican government also got involved, lobbying authorities to spare Resendiz the death penalty

"Insanity was the logical defense because no one wants to believe that there is someone out there who would do things like that," Anderson said. "That was the thing that worried me the most about the case was that jurors would just throw up their hands and say nobody in their right mind could do what he does."

"The thing about what a life sentence with Resendiz would have been, he would have enjoyed it. I mean he would have had pen pals. He would have given interviews if they let him, I mean he would have loved it. And I knew that. And he didn't deserve to live after what he did just didn't. He caused so much pain, so much heartache and so much terror, that's what the whole focus of the trial had to be."

George Benton, the husband of Claudia, would vehemently criticize the Mexican government who support his appeals and domestic opposition to the death penalty.

"(He)looked like a man and walked like a man. But what lived within that skin was not a human being."

"He was small," Anderson said when she first saw Resendiz in the courtroom. "Maybe five- foot five. His forearms though, were roped with muscles. He was scary. Even though he was small you could feel he was dangerous. He looked like a wild animal who'd been caught."

Resendiz looked "timid" in the courtroom and spoke of himself in religious riddles. He claimed he was Jewish and didn't seem effected when he was informed that the prosecution was aiming for the death penalty.

"I don't believe in death," Resendiz, said. "I know the body is going to go to waste. But me, as a person, I'm eternal. I'm going to be alive forever."

The defense said that Resendiz' crimes were caused by head injuries, drug abuse and a family history of mental illness. He has a delusional perception of the world as he believes that he can cause earthquakes, floods, and explosions and that God told him to kill his victims whom they believed to be evil.

He made a living stealing things from his victims and having his wife sell them in Mexico. "That was his job," Anderson said. "And for recreation it was killing the people who lived in the house."

"He was a very intelligent person who worked the system and knew exactly what kinds of things to say to get that defense to work."

The jury, however, would find Resendiz guilty after one hour and forty-five minutes of deliberation.

He was sentenced to die via lethal injection.

"He made it very clear during my conversation with him that he deserves to die," Owens said.

"I want to ask if it is in your heart to forgive me," Resendiz said in his final words. "You don't have to. I know I allowed the devil to rule my life. I just ask you to forgive me and ask the Lord to forgive me for allowing the devil to deceive me. I thank God for having patience with me. I don't deserve to cause you pain. You did not deserve this. I deserve what I am getting."

Resendiz then prayed in Hebrew and Spanish before drawing his final breath.

THE MYSTERY OF GLADYS DEACON

65

JAIMI FOSTER

Gladys Deacon- later called Gladys Duchess of Marlborough- was an eccentric socialite from the Gilded Age, who in later life is notable for her complete seclusion from society. A renowned beauty, Gladys captivated high society and set her sights on marrying into royalty- which, eventually, she did. But she was unstable, unhappy and erratic; after her husband died, she became a complete recluse, refusing to talk to anybody, to the point of lowering her housekeeper a key on a piece of string through an upstairs window whenever she needed to clean.

After she was evicted from the grounds of Blenheim Palace, where she had lived with her husband, she disappeared. Nobody knew where she had gone. But that wasn't the end of her story, as she was tracked down by a young author intent on learning more about her life, which had been all but forgotten.

Gladys' early life: signs of what was to come?

Gladys' early life was anything but stable. In fact, it could certainly be described as ominous, and Gladys' future behavior could certainly be explained by her tough early years. She was born Gladys Marie Deacon in Paris, way back in 1881, to relatively successful parents. They were American emigrants: her father was Edward Parker Deacon, and his wife Florence, had settled in Paris before they had their daughter. After they had Gladys, they travelled around Europe.

Florence was the daughter of Rear Admiral Charles H. Baldwin, who was famously chosen to represent the United States at Tsar Alexander III's coronation, but had refused to attend because he was not given a good enough seat. Gladys' father Edward had come from Boston, where his family had been relatively successful. To this day stands the house, Deacon House, named after his family.

The couple were unfortunate parents, despite desperately wanting to start a family. They tried and tried again to have children, but three of Gladys' sisters and one of her brothers died in infancy. Perhaps it was this that led to Edward's later madness; perhaps not, although it could be understood if it had. But Gladys' grandmother, Sarah Ann Parker, had also slowly turned mad and been hospitalised. She, perhaps, or her family before her were the source of the instability which plagued the Deacon family later on.

Florence, too, was affected by the deaths of her children. She had interesting friends, who were renowned figures at the time: Bernard Berenson, Count Robert de Montesquiou, and the painter Rodin. Perhaps it was because of her heartbreak, or perhaps it was because of her connections, but she soon took a lover named Emile Abeille. Their marriage, by all accounts, had not been a happy one anyway; so it is little surprise that the unfortunate deaths of their children would have taken a toll on her. Describing Rodin in her old age, Gladys said: 'Of course he was of a very lascivious nature. You know, hands all over you.' He once gave her a sculpture, and told her: 'Don't look too much at my other work. Life has taught me what will sell.'

Either way, the fact that Florence had taken a lover drove Edward to despair- or insanity. He pursued Florence and Emile, who had left Paris and gone travelling around Europe, and finally tracked them down to the Hotel Splendide, at Cannes, in February 1892. He knew that the couple were there together, and demanded to see them, telling hotel staff that his wife was with another man. But what the hotel staff didn't know was that he was carrying a loaded gun.

Finding the pair together in their room, he took out his gun, and immediately shot Emile. He was hiding behind the sofa at the time. Edward gave himself up to police and was taken straight to jail. Emile held on through the night, but died the next morning due to his injuries. The fact that Edward had murdered his wife's lover- even the fact that his wife *had* a lover- caused a great stir among the elite social circles in and around Paris.

Gladys makes her debut

Even from a very young age, Gladys was famed for her bright blue eyes and her Hellenic profile. But combined with her eyes and beauty, she had a fierce intelligence that impressed everybody she knew. Soon after her father's death, Gladys was sent back to school, at the Convent de l'Assomption in Auteuil. But she wasn't to stay there long, as her mother quickly took her out of school and ran away with her. When Edward was released from prison just a few weeks later- he was allowed out for diplomatic reasons, and the justification that his had been a crime of passion- he went to pick his daughter up from school only to find she had been abducted some time earlier. The couple were divorced in 1893, at which time Edward sought custody of his three eldest children, and won. He promptly left the country, going back to the United States, where the family lived with Gladys for the next three years.

According to his friends, Edward was vain, and believed that his 'conjugal exploit' gave him 'a distinction for him in the eyes of fashionable New Yorkers'. This, more than anything, shows the vanity of the Gilded Age. Apparently, his friends were shocked 'by the way he talked about it before his little daughter'. Undoubtedly, such a strange upbringing would have had a huge effect on young Gladys. Unfortunately for the family, Edward very soon lost his reason completely, and was sent to the McLean Hospital in Belmont, which is near Boston. He died in 1901.

But before then, Gladys and her sisters had returned to France to find and live with their mother. The family travelled back to Europe in 1896, when Gladys was fifteen years of age. She had finished her education- what education she could have received before being abducted from school, at least- and took to the social circles that her mother and father had loved so much. As a debutante, she was a hit- she was described as a brilliant meteor of beauty, intelligence and wit, despite still being so young.

Gladys and the Duke

Gladys' mother had settled in Rome at this point, and her family joined her. She was the mistress of Prince Doria Pamphili, and the Prince allowed them to stay at the beautiful Villa Farnese, which is just north of Rome. It was while she was staying here with her family that Gladys had an early version of cosmetic surgery performed, which she hoped would straighten out her nose. When she was 22, she underwent an operation where paraffin wax was injected into her nose; but the surgery was not a success, and the wax slipped down into her jaw where it stayed for the rest of her life. So, rather than give her a Grecian profile to enhance her beautiful looks, she made her jawline blocky and unattractive.

Nevertheless, she remained popular with society everybody fell in love with Gladys. She was the beauty of her age, and men- rich, famous, and titled- vied for her attention. Prince Roffredo Caetani, the last Duke of Sermoneta, tried to woo her; Bernard Berenson, the American art historian and his wife were very fond of her. The list goes on, a long list of lords and dukes who were all convinced of her beauty and charm. She did for a very brief time commit to an engagement with Count Hermann Keyserling, a Baltic philosopher. But their time together was torrid and unhappy, and the pair grew tired of the idea of staying together.

The Crown Prince of Prussia fell in love with Gladys, too. According to Mr Vickers, Gladys' biographer later in life: "He took one look at her and fell madly in love with her. When they were driving to Oxford in a carriage he kept turning around to the consternation of everybody, in order to gaze at Ms Deacon sitting in the back seat." He even gave her a ring which belonged to his father, the Kaiser- who demanded that it be returned. But there was nothing that any of these potential lovers could do, since Gladys had eyes only for one man.

It was around this time that Gladys first read of the Duke of Marlborough's marriage to Consuelo Vanderbilt, which perhaps was the marriage of the century so far- the extremely wealthy heiress of an American magnate marrying into an old English title. It was this that tempted her to the idea of marrying into the nobility; the ravishing attention that the pair had received convinced her that to marry a Duke would be the height, the pinnacle of her 'career'. She had settled on the Duke, and could accept nobody else. His marriage to Consuelo was well known, and was indeed representative, of the kind of loveless but socially advantageous marriages that were common during the early twentieth century. Consuelo Vanderbilt was, of course, the daughter of William Kissam Vanderbilt; he was the grandson of Cornelius, the founder of the famous family.

In her diary, Gladys was forthcoming about her jealousy towards Conseulo, and revealed that she would have dearly loved to marry the Duke herself. 'O dear me,' she wrote, 'if only I was a little older I might "catch" him yet! But Hélas! I am too young though mature in the arts of woman's witchcraft and what is the use of one without the other? I will have to give up all chance to ever get Marlborough'. Little did she know that it wouldn't take her as long as she might have thought.

Consuelo, as her marriage to the Duke was being arranged, was already secretly engaged to another man. But through the influence of her mother, she was gradually won over to the idea of marrying into a title, even though she had no interest in the Duke either as a lover or as a friend. As dowry, the Duke received several million dollars- worth perhaps $70 million or more in today's money- and connection to the highest of society. But the marriage was unhappy, the pair rarely spent time together, and the Duke's eye wandered from his wife.

At this point in time, Gladys was living a bohemian lifestyle in Paris, the very center of the bohemian world. She was a regular attendee of any and all of the important social gatherings, and was immensely popular. But just before the turn of the twentieth century, in the late 1800s, the Duke of Marlborough invited Gladys to Blenheim Palace, where the couple lived. While she was briefly there, she became friends with both the Duke and his wife Consuelo. Soon after she arrived, the Duke and Consuelo decided that she could stay for a while; but Gladys and the Duke quickly began an affair.

Gladys continued living with the Duke for many years, all the way through the Duke's divorce with Consuelo Vanderbilt. The pair finally divorced in 1921, many years after they had effectively separated and it was common knowledge that he and Gladys were a pair. Throughout these years, Gladys became a keen artist and a gardener, and she had the gardens at Blenheim Palace beautified according to her wishes. She also picked up the hobby of breeding Blenheim Spaniels, also known as King Charles spaniels. Her husband the Duke disapproved.

When they were finally married, the ceremony and dress were elaborate and beautiful. Her bridal gown was 'of gold tissue specially woven in Italy for the occasion', announced The Times. 'The Court train is of gold tissue, and the veil, of old needle-point lace, [is] arranged like a coronet.' It was on outfit befitting a lady marrying into the nobility, which had been Gladys' dream for as long as she could remember. Unbelievably, she was 40 years old when the pair married; but they had been seeing one another for over a decade. But the good times didn't last for very long.

Gladys and the Duke's unsuccessful marriage

Gladys, perhaps because of her upbringing was not content with her life. In a letter that she wrote to the Duke, she said: "Am I not the last of the Marlborough gems? Greek in temper with a more modern dash about certain parts?" An old admirer of Gladys, the Baronne Deslandes, wrote a letter to Gladys which read: 'You make me think of a diamond. You are, I believe, cold and pure and white, and cutting like that admirable stone. For the diamond has something cruel about it, don't you think?' It would be difficult to better sum up her 'unstable streak' which tore her marriage apart.

Things began well enough, with the Duke and his new wife attending many social occasions together, and the Duke even having the ceiling in one of Blenheim Palace's rooms repainted with startling paintings of Gladys' eyes; she gave the artist a scarf which matched their colour so that he could paint them perfectly.

The couple tried, but were unsuccessful in their attempt to have children. Gladys was pregnant three times, but each time her pregnancies ended prematurely. She did not want children, and perhaps revealed her secret when she would tell younger girls: 'If you have any problems, go to the vet. That's what I always do!' Even though it had been her life's ambition, it seemed that she did not want to be tied to the Duke after all. Even shortly after her marriage, she wrote in a letter: 'I loved him, but was fearful of the marriage'.

Throughout the 1920s, their marriage deteriorated. Oxfordshire proved to be a different hunting ground to her former residences in bohemian Paris and Rome, and she alienated the more old-fashioned inhabitants of the local social circles with her eccentricities. Moreover, the Duke converted to Roman Catholicism, which changed his views on marriage and on politics, which Gladys hated discussing with him. Whenever he would bring up the subject, she would say something along the lines of: 'Oh shut up! What do you know about politics? I've slept with every Prime Minister in Europe and most Kings. You are not qualified to speak!'

In a story that was only told during her final years, at one point Gladys came down to the dinner table with a revolver in her hand. The Duke and assembled guests were startled, and asked her why she had brought it: she responded: 'Oh I don't know, I might just shoot Marlborough.' Because of her instability, and the instability of their marriage, the Duke left Gladys alone at Blenheim for two years before evicting her. She took residence in their London property, Carlton House Terrace, but she was evicted from there too.

After her move, she had the Duke tailed by a series of private investigators, to find out what he was up to now that he had his freedom. It turned out that he was seeing a series of models and younger women behind her back, despite his age; he was in his 60s at the time. Having found this out, Gladys demanded that they begin divorce proceedings, with which he happily obliged. But the Duke died in 1934, before the couple had agreed to the terms of their divorce. She had settled down first in Oxfordshire, then in a village named Chacombe, where she lived with her dogs. She began to leave the house less and less, and became yet more eccentric in her loneliness.

But she filled her house with the treasures of her past: portraits, sculptures, and her immense collection of books both new and old. Her small house could have been a museum, with paintings by Degas, Toulouse Lautrec, Rodin and Boldini hanging on the walls. Her jewels, which she treasured, included a tiara that had belonged to the Imperial family itself. Whether she felt comforted in her loneliness by the fact that her house was filled with treasures- and treasures they were, since they would have cost an awful lot of money were the brought to market- we cannot know.

Tracking Gladys down

Gladys had become a recluse. Mr Vickers said: "She did become a complete and absolute recluse. I imagine that through her head were floating the most fantastic memories of Paris and Rome and Italy and all the wonderful people she'd known. But eventually it probably became too much for her and she became a scary person. She was threatening to shoot people who stole apples from her orchard and was ringing people in the middle of the night." She had originally bought the gun to keep in her bedroom, and keep the Duke away.

Her only link to the outside world was her Polish housekeeper, Andrei Kwiatowski, to whom she would lower her house key through the upstairs window of her home. He lived in a nearby village, but took the time to bring her food and drink, and care for her in any way she could. But in 1962, she was removed and taken to hospital. Her family, her old friends and relations, none of them knew where she had gone; she was lost to history, not least because she was determined to have as little contact with the outside world as possible.

It was at this point in the story that Hugo Vickers began to play a central role. Vickers, an author, was just 16 when he first encountered the story of Gladys Deacon; he was reading the diary of Conservative MP Henry 'Chips' Channon, who had encountered Gladys completely by accident one day in a jeweller's shop on Bond Street in 1943. According to his diary: "I saw an extraordinary marionette of a woman – or was it a man? It wore grey flannel trousers, a wide leather belt, masculine overcoat and a man's brown felt hat, and had a really frightening appearance, but the hair was golden-dyed and long."

But while he was looking- perhaps staring- at this "terrifying apparition", he suddenly realised who it was: "Gladys Marlborough, once the world's most beautiful woman, the toast of Paris, the love of Proust, the belle amie of Anatole France". But when he tried to introduce himself, "She looked at me, stared vacantly with those famous eyes that once drove men insane with desire and muttered: 'Je n'ai jamais entendu ce nom-la' [I've never heard that name]. She flung down a ruby clip she was examining and bolted from the shop."

Reading about this episode instilled an interest in Vickers that never quite went away, and he was determined to find out what had happened to the American beauty who had been the toast of European society at the turn of the century. There was, after all, no indication that she had died- but she had completely disappeared since then. Bear in mind that the story was from 1943, and Vickers was reading the diary in 1968; anything could have happened to her since then. But nevertheless, he was determined to track her down.

He told the BBC: "I went to Blenheim aged 16 in 1968 and I asked the guides about her. They said 'We don't talk about her.'" It proved to be a completely fruitless lead, and he was no closer to finding her. He even visited her last known address in 1975, a small house in a small village called Chacombe, with a population of just a few hundred. But again, he met a dead end. He asked the owner of a local pub if perhaps he knew anything of Gladys, but he told Vickers: 'She's been gone a long time.' That being said, he was directed to a hospital not far away- the landlord wasn't completely sure- but it was near Northampton, the county town. In 1975, Gladys- if she were still alive- would have been 94 years old. But the landlord was fairly sure she was.

As Vickers told the BBC, "It hadn't occurred to me that the reason she had disappeared was she was in fact in a psycho-geriatric hospital. I eventually tracked her down there and was allowed to go see her. I made friends with her and talked to her. She was still very intelligent and whilst sitting in this reclusive atmosphere she was reading the newspaper, keeping diaries, noting what was going on in the world and was as shrewd as anything."

Vickers had found a lawyer who could grant him the right to visit her, and he did just that- searching for her in nearby hospitals. It wasn't actually long until he found her, in a psycho-geriatric ward. He had never been to one, and found it disturbing as he was led down corridor after corridor by the chief nursing officer Mrs Newton. At last, they arrived at the O'Connell Ward, where Gladys lived permanently. She was sat in the green room, asleep in a chair with a piece of white linen over her face. Although she refused to talk to Vickers, he had found her: now, he could lift the lid on what had happened during her disappearance.

They quickly began to bond, sharing tea and poring over pictures. Vickers visited her 65 times over the course of two years. He kept record of how many times he had been. Over that time, she began to reveal the details of her life. Since she had become deaf- she was 94 years old after all- every question that Hugo wanted to ask her, he wrote down on a piece of paper in large capital letters so that they would be easier for her to read.

Hugo later described to the BBC just what it had meant to him to have met and talked with Gladys on so many occasions. "It's extraordinary for me to have met her in 1975 when she was born in 1881," Vickers said. "There came a day once when my son came from school aged 7 having copied the Haystacks by Monet. "I said to him that I had a friend who knew Monet and sent him into school the next day with a photo she'd taken of Monet in his garden at Giverny. So there is a lovely link there which in a way goes back."

Gladys' legacy

Hugo Vickers finally published his biography of Gladys Deacon after their many meetings, in 1979. Gladys had died only two years earlier, at the ripe old age of 96. She had eventually succumbed to the same mental health issues that her father and her grandmother had suffered from towards the end of their lives, and had died at St. Andrew's Hospital where she had spent the last twenty years. The biography was a modest success, and launched Hugo Vickers' writing career; he wrote a number of royal biographies on the Queen Mother, and Princess Alice of Greece.

In 2011, Blenheim Palace launched an exhibition to recognise one of their most interesting tenants. On the 15th of February, the palace opened to the public to show them artefacts from her life: photographs, paintings, letters, and even a lock of her hair. She had lived there from 1921 to 1933, after all, so there were plenty of interesting objects on display.

As part of the same exhibition, a huge bust of the 9th Duke of Marlborough- Gladys' husband- was moved from the hall into the Long Library, where the exhibition was being held. Another piece, a large waxwork of his likeness, was loaned in from Warwick Castle. Attending the exhibition were a number of the Duke's family, including the current Duke, members of the Churchill family, and Countess Gina Palffy-Szokoloczy: Gladys' great niece.

The display included a number of portraits and pictures of Gladys, as well as pictures taken *by* Gladys, particularly of the water terraces at Blenheim that she helped design. Blenheim Palace even recreated and displayed some of the costumes that Gladys and her friends wore during those years, which were a wonderful evocation of a bygone age.

THE DISAPPEARANCE OF JESSIE FOSTER

ANNIE SIMS

Disappearance of Jessie Foster

Like so many cases of missing people, the story of Jessie Foster has not ended, either happily or otherwise. Jessie Foster has been missing since 2006 and her sudden disappearance has people raising more questions than the world can answer. Many people point to her past and her shady companions, while other blame the mysterious city of Las Vegas for her missing status. Whatever the case, there leads that have been followed have all ended in dead ends.

Jessie Foster was born on May 27, 1984, to Glendene Grant and Dwight Foster. They lived in Canada and spent a lot of their time in Calgary, Alberta. Jessie herself spent most of her teen- and adult-life living in Kamloops, British Columbia. Little has been said about her personality, career, and educational level. All we know is that she was a popular athlete and an honor roll student prior to disappearing.

Jessie became missing officially in 2006 after living in Las Vegas for a little while. However, like any missing persons' case, sometimes the most important pieces of information are hidden in the days, months and even years prior to disappearing. In Jessie's case, things did appear strange to family members and friends who were silently watching over her.

When Jessie moved back to Kamloops, British Columbia, she soon got back in contact with a close friend from high school: Donald Vaz. Not long after settling in to Kamloops, Vaz invited Jessie to come with him to Fort Lauderdale, Florida, to meet his mother for unexplained reasons. This was odd because his mother was living in Edmonton, Alberta, at the time.

In early 2005, Dwight would constantly suggest to his daughter to relax and take time off of her busy work schedule to travel. Jessie would initially brush these suggestions away with reasons for meeting deadlines or having too much work to do. However, she finally relented and became much more open to the suggestion of traveling the world.

Vaz's invitation to see Florida was an excellent place to start, and she found no reason to reject.

It was in Jessie's nature to be trusting of people; that's one of the things that her parents usually faulted her for. When her friend asked her to accompany him to Florida, she didn't hesitate to accept the invitation. Not everyday do you have a reason to go to the warm south to escape chilly Canada, even if it's just for a couple weeks. And it's even rarer that you get the chance to travel for free since Vaz offered to pay for tickets, lodging, and food.

Jessie just brought her necessities with her and hopped onto the plane headed for Fort Lauderdale. After they returned to Canada, Jessie stayed for a little while in Kamloops before Vaz invited her to take a second trip to Manhattan, New York. After being offered a second trip by her high school friend to another country, this should've been the first warning sign for Jessie. However, her overly trusting nature told her to go to Vaz and see the Big Apple.

From New York, they went to Atlantic City, New Jersey. However, there was a fight between the high school friends which put a delay on their plans to return home. During their stay in New Jersey, she contacted both her mother and father (separated at the time) and told them of her situation and how she would handle it. Both her parents told retold phone conversations with Jessie with significant discrepancies.

Glendene – Jassie's mother – recalled the conversation she had with her daughter when they were stranded in New Jersey. "Jessie told me that her and Donald had a fight in their hotel room because she had lost all his money gambling and he wanted her to prostitute herself so he can get some money."

Glendene offered to pay for her trip home via Ontario. "She called me later and said everything was fine and then she called me the next day to say she was going to come home via Las Vegas instead of Toronto. She said her 21st birthday was in two weeks and she wanted to go visit her friend, Yvonne in Las Vegas and perhaps stay there for her birthday."

It's very common for new 21-year olds from Canada to visit Las Vegas to spend their birthdays so to Glendene nothing was out of the ordinary. Although disappointed that she remained with Vaz through the whole ordeal, she was glad that her daughter had everything planned out. However, one detail of their trip was either intentionally unmentioned during her phone conversations with her mom. "She told me she did NOT go to Atlantic City, New Jersey, on this trip." Jessie retold the story to her sister, Crystal, and basically said the same things she told her mom, except she mentioned that they did in fact go to New Jersey.

The version she told her father, Dwight, had different details in comparison to Glendene's and Crystal's versions. "She told me that her friend lost all his money gambling," Dwight recalls from his conversation with Jessie during her trip to New York and New Jersey, "and that he wanted me to 'turn a few tricks' to earn some money so they could get out of the USA and back to Canada. Jessie got mad and left the room, going to the hotel lobby and called me."

The three versions have differences in details, and so far there's no reason why she would give different accounts of the same story to three people. This is most likely the most complete information of her details with Vaz during their trip to New York, maybe New Jersey, and ultimately Nevada.

Jessie and Vaz arrived at Las Vegas, Nevada, on May 13, 2006. They soon met up with her friend, Yvonne (aka Angel), and would spend a couple nights at her place in preparation for Jessie's birthday. Her parents weren't entirely excited about the prospect of their daughter spending so much time away from home, especially after her whole argument with Vaz whom her parents were not on great terms with. Her parents requested Yvonne's phone number so they could have the contact of somebody there in case anything bad happened to Jessie.

Yvonne was a known prostitute and was previously charged with attempting to transport a minor across state borders for sexual purposes. She was also well-known in Vancouver, British Columbia, as a person who would frequent the red light districts in search of her next victim to smuggle out. Because of her shady past and obvious lack of guilt, she was deported from the country.

It should be apparent now Jessie's acquaintances aren't exactly the best of people. One tried to persuade her to prostitute herself in order to make cash to return home, and the other was known for smuggling minors past state lines. It was only a matter of time before something bad happened to Jessie, and that precise moment was coming quickly.

Peter Todd became Jessie's boyfriend during her stay in Las Vegas. Todd was the friend of Yvonne's boyfriend who was quickly introduced to Jessie. Not long after knowing each other, Jessie moved in with Todd. Jessie was to stay with Todd until her birthday where, according to their planes, they would spend the day drinking, gambling. Basically, they'd spend the whole day in a Las Vegas casino doing regular party-people things.

After weeks of knowing Todd and living in his lavish home, Jessie's parents received news that their daughter was now in police custody and was charged for prostitution. Her parents were dumbfounded by the news and thought it was impossible that someone with such a clean track record in her personal and academic life would be caught doing something so strange. Their first guess was that Todd somehow made Jessie become a prostitute, either by force or by tricking her. Jessie went to court and paid a fine of $600 since it was her first offense.

Todd was there are her hearing and paid the fine before quickly sweeping her away into his car and bringing her back home. The things that Glendene read and heard about in Las Vegas around the time her daughter moved there were worrying. "There is another woman named Lindsay Marie Harris," Glendene writes in her blog, "who went missing in May 2006, just two months before [Jessie] arrived in Las Vegas. Did they replace Lindsay with Jessie?"

According to some reports, Jessie and Lindsay had the same description, upbringing, and missing person story. In addition, Lindsay was arrested five times before suddenly vanishing into thin air. "Were Lindsay and Jessie bumped?" Glendene asks herself and her blog reader. "Were they determined to be more trouble than they were worth, to their pimps or human traffickers?" Some speculate that Lindsay and Jessie were both discovered by the same people and pushed into sex trafficking before being forcibly removed.

Glendene called Lindsay's parents, wanting to talk about the similarities between the stories of their missing daughters but only reached their voicemail. They returned the call back to Glendene and told her everything they knew about the case. At the time, Lindsay was missing for about a year and like Jessie, the North Las Vegas Police Department hardly had any leads to follow.

"[Lidnsay's mother] knew her daughter was not alive," Glendene recalls in her blog about her missing daughter, "She has never felt that Lindsay is alive. And, sadly, neither did Lindsay's twin brother." After three years, Glende heard news of Lindsay's body being found by police. Lindsay's and Jessie's DNA were compared against a body found by the police department. "She knew she wasn't alive, and she was right. The police have told me it is sometimes their best investigative tool... mother."

After several months of their relationship, Jessie and her boyfriend were engaged to get married. The whole time she was in Las Vegas, she would keep her family updated on her situation. "She would call me and Jim – her stepdad – several times a week. Same with her dad and Tracy – her stepmother. Her sisters and friends got calls and text messages several times a week but sometimes [even] several times a day."

During her ten month stay in Las Vegas, she only returned to Canada once to see her family. "It was only for a few weeks at the end of the year 2005, and we even though – hoped – she might stay in Canada, since she and Peter, her fiancé in North Las Vegas, Nevada, was now a known pimp and the person known to the police on Jessie's case." In her frequent calls to her fiancé while she was back in Canada, Jessie and Todd would argue endlessly over the phone.

"I was actually happy since it seemed they always fought," Glendene says in her blog about her missing daughter, "and now she was home and did not have to put up with it." Jessie would talk to her mother over the phone during her arguments with her fiancé, and Glendene even pleaded to Todd to let her daughter return home safely. "They would always make up and she never came home to live."

On Christmas day in 2005, Jessie was to return to Las Vegas and Todd to resume her life there. "Jessie told us we needed to drive her to the airport because she had to get back to Las Vegas to see [Todd]. It was so urgent and out of the blue, we tried to find out what was going on. She said nothing."

The following months after New Year's were pretty much repetitive for the newly engaged couple: they'd argue, Jessie would call her mom or dad, they'd make up, and everything would be fine until the next argument. There is little information on what occurred during the months after her return to Las Vegas after Christmas 2005. However, things would suddenly become a parent's worst nightmare when, out of nowhere, Jessie went missing.

The last reported sighting of Jessie was of her exiting the premises of her fiancés home with her bags in her arms, apparently packed up and ready to go. There was no sighting of Todd, and there is speculation that the couple's constant bickering finally forced Jessie to take matters into her own hands and leave.

After this occurrence, Jessie went missing the North Las Vegas Police Department reported finding three other women. All of them, including Jessie herself, were known prostitutes living and working in North Las Vegas. As soon as the bodies were found, the police launched an immediate investigation to find the killer or anyone involved in the killing of the three women.

After discovering that their daughter was missing, Glendene and Dwight automatically pointed fingers at Todd as the person to blame for their missing daughter. The police took Todd into custody and interrogated him regarding Jessie's whereabouts and what the magnitude of their relationship was. Surprisingly, Todd was clean and had seemingly had no reason to cause harm on his fiancé. The police let him go but felt compelled to interrogate him again after a clue in Jessie's missing case brought them back to Todd. The police searched his home and his belongings but nothing was found that could pin Todd as a responsible party for her disappearance. Again, the police released him and he was no longer a suspect.

After three years of grasping at straws, Glendene and Dwight are unable to blame Todd, Vaz, or even Yvonne on their missing daughter. Things were suspicious from the start, especially with Vaz who took their daughter to Fort Lauderdale, Florida, under false pretenses of meeting his mother. There was absolutely no reason for him to lie to Jessie, seeing as how she would've traveled with an old high school friend to sunny Floridian beaches in a heartbeat.

Yvonne, the friend living is Las Vegas who was charged with selling a minor for sex purposes, is another shady character that, for reasons unknown, managed to befriend Jessie and maintain that relationship long enough that Jessie would come to Las Vegas and stay with her in preparation for her birthday. Even knowing her dubious past, Jessie could still trust her enough to live with her and meet her mutual friends. This leads to Peter Todd who was the last person to ever have a significant relationship with Jessie before leaving.

What hold did Todd have on Jessie that made her absolutely have to leave for Las Vegas during Christmas day 2005? Was she deeply in love with Todd that she was his puppet? Was he threatening her over the phone to do something to her if she didn't return? Was Jessie's family threatened? Why are Glendene and Dwight so sure that Todd is involved in making their daughter disappear when even the police can't find any evidence that would suspect him of any wrongdoing?

Ever since Jessie disappeared that day in Las Vegas, the course of Glendene's and Dwight's lives changed. There's nothing more devastating to a parent than losing a child and not knowing what happened to them. They're not a part of the what-ifs and body watches community. They get on the edge of their seats whenever the remains of a person are discovered.

In the beginning, both her parents were constantly stressed about what possible torture their daughter would be going through. The mystery of their missing daughter was like an open wound that wouldn't heal. The continuous train of thought about any and every possible bad thing to happen to their daughter had crossed their mind.

During the first year of Jessie's disappearance, Glendene refused to leave her house and even allowed her food stock to run dry several times. She was constantly grieving over the loss of her daughter whilst raising the daughters who remained in Canada. She left her job and dedicated her time and resources into finding what happened to her beloved daughter who left for Las Vegas so many years ago.

Both Glendene and Dwight hired a private investigator that frequently traveled to Las Vegas to search the entire city for their daughter. Unfortunately, the private investigator found nothing – no clues, no rumors, no ideas, and no Jessie. It seemed as if everything that could go wrong went wrong. However, the private investigator did uncover some historical information regarding their daughter that they were unaware of before. Apparently, Jessie had been hospitalized with a broken jaw and arrested twice for prostitution.

Then, near the end of the first year of Jessie's disappearance, Glendene received a signal that caused her to continue her search for Jessie. While on a flight to Las Vegas to do some of her own personal searching, she learned that police in Missouri had found Sean

Hornsbeck – a child who was kidnapped – after four years of searching. Though four years was still much too long for Glendene to wait, it was better than nothing. She grasped onto that ray of hope and set a goal of finding her daughter within the first four years of her search.

However, it's been 11 years now and no new leads have surfaced that could unite Glendene and Dwight with their missing daughter. In 2015, there were reports that a man found dead in Oregon could possibly be linked to what happened to Jessie so many years ago. The man succumbed to fatal gunshot wounds when a prostitute pulled the trigger in self defense. The man was being investigated to ties with several unsolved cases including prostitutes, and even one that involves a Calgary woman.

"I do believe Jessie is alive," Glendene told reporters after hearing of the Oregon man's ill fate, "But I want answers, and not only the ones I wanted. I will accept what happened to Jessie and I will go on. If this is what [the Oregon man] was doing 10 years ago, there is a possibility... [If Jessie's dead], it is more likely this type of person did something to her." Dwight never commented on the case of the murdered man from Oregon, mainly due to his deep depression stemming from his missing daughter.

"The dark thoughts come in – you close your eyes for a few minutes – and your thoughts invariably go to my daughter," he told reporters in a previous interview, "I don't even want to think about it because those are thoughts that rip you to pieces."

The only information available about Jessie in Las Vegas are depressing and causes Glendene to become less hopeful of her daughter's return. Jessie's hospital records suggest that she was involved with a ring of violent people in Las Vegas. The subsequent reports of Jessie's involvement in prostitution were like fitting two pieces of a puzzle together. "It's like all of a sudden I realized, taken to another country, beaten and forced into the sex trade – yeah, that's exactly what that is." Meanwhile, Dwight believes that his daughter – a highly ambitious person with deep love for money and the good life – may have willingly entered the profession in order to fulfill any new addictions she picked up in Las Vegas.

11 years later, without any idea about the whereabouts of their missing daughter, Glendene and Dwight still dwell on this mysterious missing persons case. However, they both have different ways of dealing with the depression and psychological scars.

Dwight mainly holds onto the issue himself and rarely speaks of his daughter out of fear of reopening emotional wounds. He's still living with his family, but at times he can seem distant and unwilling to socialize. He spends his nights awake in his study, constantly thinking and reminiscing of his missing daughter. He's no longer the happy guitar-playing father he was before the incident that caused his daughter to leave his life. A father who's missing a daughter with whom he was extremely close to can easily close himself off from the outside world.

Meanwhile, Glendene has taken another approach of dealing with her depression. Instead of staying indoors and out of sight, she started Mothers Against Trafficking Humans, a non-profit organization dedicated to helping reunite families suffering from past sex trafficking crimes, in her daughter's name. Glendene has taken it upon herself to dedicate time and money to the cause and feels a vicarious happiness when broken families can become whole again.

Early on in the case, a detective advised Glendene not to try and make this a national issue since "no one would be interested in Jessie's story." Glendene didn't take that sitting down and immediately ran multiple campaigns to raise awareness of the very real, very dangerous problem of human trafficking. Jessie's story has appeared in numerous documentaries, bookies and newspapers. Glendene is also invited to many high schools and universities each year to talk about her missing daughter and speak about sex trafficking.

"I don't lose hope," Glendene said in an interview regarding her missing daughter and the organization she helms, "but I don't dream about the what-ifs. Those are the ones that will put you in the psych ward." When asked about what she thinks of Dwight's coping mechanism, she appears sympathetic. "Somewhere in his dad mind, he probably felt that he didn't protect her."

One day, after 10 years of searching, Glendene was alerted by police that a homeless woman was found intoxicated and had a very slight resemblance to her young 21-year old daughter. Glendene has had her spirits lift to the sky and brought down to hell before, and she knew she shouldn't get her hopes up. But something about the call made her truly believe that the homeless woman might be her daughter.

At around midnight the police were still doing their regular tests on their late-night detainees, and the fingerprint scan results were almost done. In the meantime, Metro Police called Glendene and told her of the situation. Earlier that night, Metro Police found the woman and wouldn't respond to any questions, including their line of questions regarding Jessie Foster. The police took three pictures of the woman and sent them to Glendene.

Looking at the photographs, the first two pictures were not even remotely close to the facial features of her missing daughter. But something in the third picture caused her to remember her daughter and show a positive sign that this homeless woman might very well be the daughter she has fought 11 years to find.

In order to draw a clear conclusion, the police gave the phone to the homeless woman to speak with Glendene. Glendene asked a number of questions but received no response. She became angry with the homelass person for her lack of cooperation and understanding, but the fingerprint scans were complete and conclusive. This woman, who has a very slight resemblance to Jessie Foster in one of her pictures taken by a police offer whilst she was intoxicated, was unequivocally not the Glendene's missing daughter.

"I wanted it to be her," Glendene said hopelessly as she received the report. The heart and soul can only take so much of a pounding before the body decides to retreat into the recesses of a dark, empty room with nothing for company except old pictures and memories. Again, it happened to Glendene and again she has to pick up what remaining hope she has to continue the search for her daughter. The next day, the search for Jessie Foster continued.

If anybody has any information about the possible whereabouts of Jessie Foster (now aged 34) who was last seen in Las Vegas, Nevada, please inform the North Las Vegas Police Department or Calgary Police Force of Alberta. The latest reward offered for any information leading to the successful finding of Jessie Foster was $50,000. A hope-filled mother and depressed father eagerly await the day where their beloved daughter can return to their arms safe and sound, or where they can finally receive the closure they have been in search of since 2006.

MISSING BEAUMONT CHILDREN

It was a warm summer morning on January 26, 1966, when the three Beaumont children left their suburban home to celebrate Australia Day at the beach. The children regularly made the trip by themselves, so their mother felt at ease providing them with bus fare and sending them on their way while she visited and had lunch with a close friend. However, she would return home that afternoon to find that the children still had not returned. That morning would end up being the last time she saw her three children.

Jane (aged 9), Arnna (aged 7), and Grant (aged 4), lived in Somerton Park, a quiet suburb minutes away from Adelaide, South Australia. Their father, Jim Beaumont, was a linen goods salesman who frequently traveled for work and their mother, Nancy Beaumont, was a stay-at-home mother.

The oldest child, Jane, was viewed by her parents as responsible enough to supervise the other children for short trips and adventures, a style of parenting that was the norm in Australia at that time. The children frequently took the five-minute bus ride to neighboring Glenely Beach by themselves and were looking forward to celebrating the national holiday at the beach.

The children left their home at 10:00am that morning and were seen arriving at the beach by witnesses at 10:15am. They spent much of that morning at play on the beach and were supposed to arrive home at 2:00pm. When they did not arrive at the appointed time, their mother assumed that they had become preoccupied with celebrating the holiday with their playmates and that they would arrive on the next bus or had decided to walk home, something that the three children had done before. When the children did not disembark from the next scheduled bus, their mother began to grow worried.

The disappearance of the Beaumont children would result in one of the largest manhunts and police investigations in Australian history. Furthermore, the event had widespread consequences on Australian society, shattering the illusion that many parents had regarding their children's safety and changing the way that Australians parented their children forever.

Timeline of Events

10:00am - The children leave their Somerton Park home to travel to Glenely Beach by bus.

10:15am - They are seen exiting the bus by multiple witnesses.

11:00am - The three children are spotted playing beneath a sprinkler by an elderly woman. A tall blond man is spotted lying on the ground next to them, watching the children play.

11:15am - A tall blond man is seen playing with the children. They all appear to be laughing and at ease.

11:45am - The children purchase several pastries and a meat pie from the beach snack shop.

12:15pm - The tall blond man and the children are seen leaving the beach together. The children are witnessed laughing together and holding hands.

3:00pm - A postman on his route spots the children walking along Jetty Road alone, away from the beach. The postman is known to the children and they exchange greetings. Police believe that the timeline for this event is incorrect.

7:20pm - The parents of the children become gravely concerned and file a missing children's report with the local police department. Jim Beaumont and the local police search the entire Glenely Beach area.

8:40pm - Police search the surrounding beaches with no results. The father contacts friends and relatives in an attempt to locate the children.

10:00pm - Police issue public radio announcements with a missing children report.

Points of Interest

There are several details in this story which raised doubts with both the parents of the children and the local police department. When the children departed for Glenely Beach in the morning of January 26th, they left with only enough money to cover their bus fare: six shilling and a sixpence. However, the shop owner, who sold several pastries and a meat pie to the children at 11:45am, reported that the children paid for the food with a $1 bill, an amount of money that they did not have when they left their mother's care.

In addition, the shop owner knew the children well and had sold them food and pastries several times before. He reported that the children had never purchased a meat pie before. This suggests that the children received the money from someone after leaving their parents home and that they may have been purchasing the meat pie for someone else.

Lastly, the mother of the children, Nancy Beaumont, repeatedly said that her children were quite shy and very unlikely to speak with strangers, indicating that they may have met the tall blond man prior to the date of their disappearance. Their mother also remembered a seemingly innocuous comment from Arnna, who had previously told her mother that Jane had "got a boyfriend down the beach." Nancy assumed that her daughter was referring to a young playmate, but in hindsight it seems that she may have been referring to the tall blond man spotted by witnesses.

Police Investigation

The South Australian police force began investigating the disappearance of the children in full-force the evening of their disappearance. After interviewing several witnesses who were present at Glenely Beach, they were able to determine that the children were playing with a tall blond, "thin-faced" man while at the beach. He was described as being a blond man in his late 30s with a thin or athletic build.

"Things seemed bungled from the get-go," forensic psychologist Paula Orange said. "First off, the artist drawing the picture admitted to being drunk at the time of completing his task. So the sketch made of the suspect looks more like a lantern-jawed alien than a real person. Secondly, the witnesses claimed that the man was in his late thirties. Witnesses are notorious for getting ages wrong and the police dismissed too many possible subjects out of hand because they didn't fit the profile."

Several witnesses stated that the man was seen dressing the children prior to leaving the beach. The children's parents said that the kids, especially Jane, were very shy and unlikely to speak to a stranger. This later led police to theorize that the children had met the man in question prior to the date of their disappearance and had grown to know him over a period of several weeks.

The blond man and three children were seen leaving the beach together at 12:15pm, after the children purchased several pastries and a meat pie from a local vendor with a $1 bill, an amount of money that they did not have when they left their home that morning.

A wrench was thrown into the investigation when a postman, who knew the children and was on friendly terms with them, reported that he saw the children around 3:00pm that afternoon walking away from the beach and in the direction of their home in Somerton Park. He stated that he exchanged greetings with the young children and that they seemed to be in good spirits. In particular, the postman said that he say the children were "holding hands and laughing" as they walked down the road alone, with no blond companion in sight. Police later said that they believed the postman was mistaken about the timeline and that he most likely saw the children walking some time before noon.

Several months later, a woman in a nearby neighborhood contacted police and told them that she had seen a man with two girls and a young boy enter an abandoned house on her street. She also reported seeing the young boy walking away from the house before he was roughly grabbed by, and returned to the house with, the older man. She never saw the man or children again.

"The response from the public was overwhelming," Orange said. "People drove from miles away to aid in the search. They combed the beach and drained part of it all to no avail. They found nothing, not a trace."

The police were quickly able to eliminate drowning as the cause of the children's disappearance as a result of several witnesses saying that they saw the children leave the beach around 12:15pm. Furthermore, all of the children's belongings were missing, lending further support to the theory that they left the beach. After speaking with the parents, the police were able to identify seventeen different items that were carried by the children that day, providing a list of items that could be used to identify their remains or whereabouts. However, the police's continue efforts continued to prove fruitless.

The Psychic Circus

On November 8, 1966, nearly a year after the children's initial disappearance, an internationally-renowned psychic from the Netherlands, Gerard Croiset, was flown to Australia to investigate the case. His presence caused a whirlwind of media coverage in Australia and across the world. After making a series of outlandish and ever-changing claims, Croiset claimed that the children were buried underneath a warehouse just minutes away from the children's school.

"I appreciate him (Gerard Croiset) coming out to find the children," Jim Beaumont said. "But I don't believe what he said. I don't believe the children are dead and will continue to believe until given evidence that proves otherwise."

The building, which was under construction at the time of their disappearance, was eventually razed and excavated after the owners raised $40,000 for the project as a result of public pressure. No evidence of the children or their belongings were ever found.

"The press and police followed Croiset around everywhere," Orange said. "He was an obvious con artist but they were desperate. They had nothing."

A Series of Letters

Beginning in 1968, the parents of the three children began to receive a series of letters which rekindled hope in the idea that their children may still be alive. Postmarked from Dandernong, Victoria, the series of letters claimed to be written by Jane, the eldest daughter. She claimed to be under the supervision of a man and in good health and care, saying

Dear Mum and Dad,

We had a beautiful lunch today...The man is feeding us really well. The man took us to see The Sound of Music yesterday.

Police officers believed the letters to be from Jane after comparing them to examples of her handwriting and, as far as 1981, the Sidney Morning Herald produced analysis from handwriting experts claiming that the letters were actually from the missing child.

Following receipt of the letters supposedly sent from Jane, the parents received a letter from a man claiming to be in possession of the children. He said that he was willing to hand the children over to the parents at a specific time and location. The Beaumonts arrived at the appointed time and location with an undercover police officer but no one showed. They later received a letter from the same man claiming that he saw the undercover police officer arrive with the parents and that he would now keep the children, ending any hope of a peaceful exchange.

In 1992, following another investigation and remarkable achievements in fingerprint technology, authorities identified the author of the letters as a local man who was just a teenager at the time of the hoax. He reportedly wrote and mailed the letters as "a joke."

False Closure

Then, in November 2013, South Australian police received an anonymous tip claiming that the children were buried underneath a warehouse located in North Plympton. Although radar identified "one small anomaly, which can indicate movement or objects within the soil," no evidence was ever found.

The Suspects

Bevan Spencer von Einem

Bevan Spencer von Einem has long been considered the prime suspect in the disappearance of the Beaumont children. Einem was convicted of the July 1983 murder of fifteen-year-old Richard Kelvin, son of a popular news reporter, in 1984. Police have long suspected Einem of working with a series of accomplices and of having committed other abductions and murders.

In 1983, a police informant known as "Mr. B" told police that Einem claimed to have taken three children from a beach to perform medical "experiments," claiming that he performed "brilliant surgery" on the three children before accidentally killing one of them. Following the child's accidental death, the informant stated that Einem claimed to have killed the other two children and buried them in an open field outside the city of Adelaide.

Einem did bare some resemblance to the descriptions of the tall blond man given to police following the disappearance of the Beaumont children and was known to frequent Glenely Beach to spy on people in the changing rooms. He was also noted as having an obsession with children.

Einem worked as an accountant and lived with his mother. There were rumors that he was part of a ring of Adelaide professionals who shared a "hobby" of kidnapping, drugging and raping boys.

"Einem did match the description of the police sketches," Orange said. "And he did like to frequent the same beach. He seemed more interested in young teenage males as his list of known victims would indicate. Einem was a homosexual who picked up hitchhikers with his transvestite friend where they would engage in a "rough trade" style of sex. He would take photographs of his victims as a keepsake. The three young children would seem to be outside of his modus operandi."

However, Einem was significantly younger than the suspect described by witnesses; Einem was around 20 years old at the time, while the description of the suspect placed him in his late 20s. But, in 2007 local police officers identified a young man who looked exactly like a young Einem in Channel 7 news footage of the incident taken days after the disappearance. He remains a prime suspect in the case.

"The newly found news footage does implicate Einem in a psychological way," Orange said. "Killers often like to return to the scene of the crime. He was spotted on film, days after the disappearance. What are the odds against that?"

Arthur Stanley Brown

Arthur Stanley Brown, along with Einem, is considered to be one of two prime suspects in the abduction of the Beaumont children. In 1988, Brown, then 86 years old, was charged with kidnapping, raping, and murdering Judith and Susan Mackey in Townsville, Queensland. His first trial was declared a mistrial after the jury failed to reach a verdict in the case and his second trial was blocked because he was declared unfit to stand trial; Brown was suffering from dementia and Alzheimer's disease by this time.

He is considered one of two prime suspects in the case because of his connection to the murder of other children and because of his remarkable resemblance to descriptions of the tall blond man seen with the children at the time of their disappearance. He was also a prime suspect in the Adelaide Oval case, which involved the disappearance of Joanna Ratcliffe and Kirste Gordon.

"Brown was a known pedophile by his closest family members," Orange said. "He is alleged to have molested numerous younger relatives. He could be placed in the same area and time of the Beaumont children but nothing could be proven."

Although Brown is considered to be a prime suspect in the disappearance of the Beaumont children, the suspect in the case was identified as being in his late 30s; Brown was in his 50s at the time. Brown died in 2002 without ever admitting to the crime.

"Brown would move into a nursing home at the end of his life," Orange said. "He would die an innocent man with the courts never able to officially charge him because of his Alzheimer's."

James Ryan O'Neill

James Ryan O'Neill, convicted of murdering nine-year-old Ricky John Smith in the Australian state of Tasmania in 1975 and currently serving a life sentence for the crime, was considered as a suspect in the Beaumont children disappearance for some time. He is reported as having told several friends in the early 1970s that he was responsible for the disappearance of the Beaumont children in 1966. However, he was publicly eliminated as a suspect by the South Australian police. He remains in prison in Tasmania to this day.

"O'Neill was the subject of a documentary called 'The Fishermen,'" Orange said. "In the documentary, he is evasive about being the man behind the disappearance of the children. He is, however, at the forefront of most pundits who have studied the story. While Brown and Einem did not have charming personas, O'Neill did. He was handsome and smiley with the ability to manipulate everyone around him. He could fabricate lies at the drop of a hat so it is easy to believe that he would be able to charm the children into his acquaintance. People who knew him all described him as 'the most likable man you'll ever meet.' No one could believe that he would be capable of such an act."

Derek Ernest Percy

In 2007, the Victorian newspaper The Age published a report stating that Derek Ernest Percy, at the time the longest-serving prisoner in the southeastern Australian state, was responsible for the disappearance of the Beaumont children in 1966. Initially jailed in

1970 for the 1969 murder of 12-year-old Yvonne Tuohy, Percy was found not guilty of the crime by reason of insanity, but was nonetheless jailed "indefinitely."

He is widely considered to be Australia's worst child serial killer and is suspected of the killings of the Beaumont children, as well as the abduction, attempted rape, and stabbing of Marianne Schmidt and Christine Sharrock on January 11, 1965. In October 2014, Percy was also ruled to have abducted and killed seven-year-old Linda Stilwell in 1968. However, Percy passed away from cancer in 2013, having never admitted to any of his crimes. He remains a possible suspect in the case.

"Percy is unique in that he may have had his mother not aiding him but covering up for him," Orange said. "He is certainly one of the most sadistic pedophiles on record, his doings are unmentionable out of respect for his victims. He was in the city at the time of the Beaumont children disappearance and is probably the top suspect along with O'Neill. His mother, however, has thrown out a lot of what could have been evidence in the case."

Related Cases

Two similar cases to the disappearance of the Beaumont children attracted widespread attention in the South Australian media, and the primary suspect in the Beaumont children's kidnapping case was convicted in one case and suspected in the other.

The Adelaide Oval Case

On August 25, 1972, two young girls, Joanne Ratcliffe (aged 11) and Kirste Gordon (aged 4) went missing while attending an Australian football game. They are presumed dead. This case also received widespread attention in the South Australian media and Bevan Spencer von Einem was considered the primary suspect in their disappearance.

Einem matched the descriptions of the tall blond man provided by witnesses in the Beaumont children's case and closely resembles the police sketch released to the public. A private police report in leaked in 1989 identified Einem as the primary suspect in the case.

The Family Murders

From 1973 to 1983, a group of men is believed to have been involved in the abduction, rape, and murder of a series of young men and male teenagers in the Adelaide area. Five teens were killed during this time period, including Alan Barnes (aged 16), Neil Muir (aged 25), Peter Stogneff (aged 14), Mark Langley (aged 18), and Richard Kelvin (aged 15). All victims were abducted and subjected to extended bouts of torture and physical assault, including sexual assault and medical experimentation.

Bevan Spencer von Einem was convicted of the abduction and murder of Richard Kelvin 1984 and is currently serving life in prison in Port Augusta prison. In 1990, he was also charged with the murder of Alan Barnes and Mark Langley, but key evidence from the Richard Kelvin murder was ruled inadmissible in the trial. Following the ruling against this key evidence, the prosecution dropped these charges against Einem on December 21, 1990.

Although Einem was the only member of this group to be convicted, and four out of five of The Family Murders remain unsolved, law enforcement officials believe that Einem was part of a white-collar group that preyed on young children. He remains the prime, and only living, suspect in the disappearance of the Beaumont children.

Impact on the Parents

Jim and Nancy Beaumont continued to hold out hope of finding their children for several decades after their disappearance. In fact, the couple continued to live at the Somerton Park home, at 109 Harding Street, that they shared with their children for nearly two decades, hoping that the children would return home someday. Nancy Beaumont was reported as saying that it would be "dreadful" if the children returned to the home only to find that their parents had moved.

"The Beaumonts left the rooms of the children untouched," Orange said. "Every toy, every book even the bed was left exactly as the children had left them."

The couple were never considered as suspects in the case and cooperated with the police at every turn in the investigation, including working with the police and searching in vain every time a new lead developed in the case over the next several decades.

According to The Age, the parents "have since separated, but still live in Adelaide." The stress and sorrow that resulted from their children's abduction, combined with the constant new leads and media attention is said to have contributed to the failure of their marriage.

Jim, in particular, is said to still be suffering from intense and inconsolable grief every time a new development is reported. Nancy was also reported to have suffered extreme grief and horror when, in 1990, several Australian newspapers released computer-generated images of what her children would look like after aging several decades. She reportedly refused to look at the pictures.

"Jim was a little bit stronger than Nancy," Orange said. "He would address the media more than she did. But they both suffered terribly for the rest of their lives into their eighties. They would spend over fifty years wishing for their children's return, getting false hope after false hope, one false lead after another which would all ultimately turn up nothing. It was a horrific cruelty."

Lastly, Jim and Nancy have largely been seen as sympathetic and pitiable figures in the Australian media and in society at large. Although their actions may seem reckless or irresponsible by today's standards, Australian society was viewed as extremely safe in the 1960s and their policy of allowing a child to supervise their younger siblings both in the home and in public was practiced by a large portion of Australian parents.

Impact on Australian Society

The disappearance of the Beaumont children became an overnight sensation in Australia, led to one of the largest police searches in the country's history, and remains the most famous missing persons case in the country. Prior to this incident, Australia was largely viewed as one of the safest societies on the planet and children were allowed to roam freely, doors remained unlocked at all times, and there was little fear of strangers. All of that changed overnight.

"Australia lost its innocence with the disappearance of the Beaumont Children," Orange said. "For three young children to disappear was unheard of. The city where they grew up was a dignified place, a safe place. But it was all an illusion that went away the day the children went missing."

During the initial search for the children, Jim Beaumont went on national television to appeal for their safe return. His heartfelt address to the nation had a lasting impact on the parents and children who watched his plea. Hundreds of viewers called into the station to offer tips and Australian police report that hundreds of tips continue to come in every year to this day. His image on national television continues to serve as a warning for those who believe in the incorruptibility of their fellow citizens and in the safety of their country.

"A lot of people today will blame the parents for letting them go on the bus alone," Adelaide resident Rachel Harding said. "But times were different back then. Back then kids would walk to school by themselves. Kids were told not to talk to strangers. The Beaumonts did tell their children to not talk to children. But child molesters are cunning monsters. My guess is that he may have stolen the eldest child's purse then conned them into seeing him as their benefactor. They would not have had money to get home then along comes this "blonde man" who offers them money. Buys them food and promises to take them home."

Children who came of age in Australia during the 1960s have remarked that there was a definite culture shift following the Beaumont children's disappearance, often describing a "before" and "after." While children were once allowed to roam freely and interact with strangers, Australian parents have since altered their style of parenting and curtailed the amount of freedom offered to young children.

"It was the type of case where we believe there was a lone offender," Australian police detective Des Bray said. "It isn't the type of crime where one would go around bragging about. But we do hope that he told someone and that somebody knows something."

If the Beaumont children are alive today, they would all be in their 50s and would have lived through years of hearing their names and story broadcast on national television and reported on breathlessly in national newspapers. Despite the vast amount of information we have on the case, their fates may never be known with any certainty.

Both Jim and Nancy Beaumont are still alive, and as of this writing they are ninety and eighty-years old respectively. The anonymous tips and false hopes continue to come in today as they did over fifty years ago.

THE MISSING BEAUTY QUEEN : THE DISAPPEARANCE OF TARA GRINSTEAD

AMANDA DARLING

"I'm an 11th-grade history teacher at Irwin County High school. I also have a cheerleading squad of Junior Varsity cheerleaders. I just completed my first year of teaching, and I love every bit of it." - Tara Grinstead in a 1999 interview.

Tara Grinstead was a beauty pageant winner and high school teacher who strangely disappeared on October 22nd, 2005.

The mystery of her disappearance is as baffling now as it was over ten years ago. Tara was a beautiful woman in a small town and drew the attention of many men. But as investigators peeled back the onion on her life, they discovered that she had a complex personal life, one with many lovers and layers of relationship any one of whom may have sought to do her harm out of jealousy.

Investigators have pieced together the timeline of her activities prior to her disappearance. But the missing piece lies sometime during the night of October 22nd, 2005, when someone abducted Tara Grinstead and she would never be seen again.

What happened to Tara Grinstead?

EARLY LIFE

Tara was born on November 14th, 1974 to Faye and Billy Grinstead. She grew up in Hawkinsville, Georgia and was a popular cheerleader in high school as well as a diligent student. Her parents would divorce and her father would remarry a woman named Connie to whom Tara grew close to as well.

Tara loved animals, singing and going to church as a kid.

One cannot look upon pictures and video of Tara and not remark that she had a striking beauty. Graced with a voluptuous figure and long black hair, she had the ability to light up any room she walked into. She would eventually compete in beauty pageants, falling in love with the preparation, competition, and glamor of the activity.

"She had been into so many (pageants) that I had lost count," Connie Grinstead said.

Tara meticulously prepared for the pageants, remaining physically fit, taking speech lessons and learning how to sing. She would also graduate from Middle Georgia College and become a teacher at Irwin County High School in Ocilla. She would teach history to 11th graders but not give up on her pageant hopes.

In 1999, she would achieve the first step in her dream to enter the Miss USA contest, when she would win the local title of Miss Tifton.

This victory would allow her to compete in the Miss Georgia pageant. She would also receive scholarship winnings that she would use to help pay for her continuing college education.

"It was, for her, more than a dream come true," Tara's best friend Maria Hulett said. "It was the chance for her to be really proud of herself."

Footage of Tara during the Georgia pageant showed her to be an exuberant woman with a zest for life. She loved to exercise, drink Diet Coke with grenadine, collect Barbies and listening to 80s music like Bon Jovi. She had an infectious smile and played to the camera as she showed off her yellow business suit that she would wear for the pageant interview.

"Why did you pick yellow?" the reporter asked.

"Because it shows that I'm a happy person," Tara said.

With her pageant days behind her, Tara would earn a master's degree in education from Valdosta State University.

"She wanted to be a principal," her friend Oshja Anderson said. "She was well on her way."

Always seeking to improve herself, Tara would teach classes during the day and go to graduate school at night. She also held down a part-time job selling cosmetics at the local department store. By 2005, she had applied for a doctoral program in history and would occasionally fill in as the assistant principal.

"On the surface," forensic psychiatrist Orange said. "Tara's life looked to be a stellar one. She had a bright future in academia and during her pageant days, she learned to put forward the best appearance. But what lurked underneath in her personal life is the mystery."

MARCUS HARPER

At the heart of Tara's disappearance is figuring out the type of relationships she had with the numerous men in her life. She worked as a teacher, went to night school and worked the cosmetics counter at a department store. Outgoing and bubbly, she didn't have the personality type to reject anyone out of hand. She attracted men and had many suitors.

She did have a longtime boyfriend in Marcus Harper.

Harper was an Ocilla police officer who would later become an Army Ranger. Both of Tara's parents liked him as they both expressed the fact that he always remained respectful of them. They have consistently maintained that they never witnessed Harper treating Tara with disrespect.

Tara, however, had expressed to her sister that she was afraid of Marcus.

"She said she was afraid of him," Tara's sister Anita said. "What he had gone through with the Ranger training. He was capable of anything."

"Marcus was a strong Alpha-male type," Orange said. "A cop and an Army Ranger. Tara was rumored to have dated another cop as well but she didn't appear to have a type. From what we can gather, she dated a slew of men from older to younger, and from different walks of life."

About a year prior to her disappearance, Tara had broken up with Marcus. She had given him an ultimatum and wanted to be married. He did not want marriage but wanted to remain committed. The relationship would turn sour at that point.

Tara would begin to date other people. She was in a car with a romantic suitor named Rhett Roberts who was the son of her landlord.

Marcus spotted the couple and would go ballistic, shouting obscenities at Tara.

Despite this angry confrontation, Tara would maintain ties with Marcus. In late July or early August of 2005 they would go to St. Augustine on a beach trip. After their date, Tara would confide to a friend that she was concerned about Marcus's temper.

Marcus would then be deployed back to Iraq a few weeks later. Tara would write the Army Ranger a letter in which she effectively ended their relationship.

According to Marcus, however, their relationship didn't come to a close until October of 2005. He had returned from the Middle East and called Tara to tell her that their relationship was over. Tara was at work and became so distraught that had to pull over to the side of the road. She called a friend who came and took her home. The next day, Tara would call off sick from her teaching job in order to "take a mental health day."

There was a rumor that a cop from a neighboring town, Heath Dykes, came to visit Tara at her school shortly afterward.

"These behaviors certainly show some mental fragilities on the parts of both Tara and Marcus," Orange said. "From what we can gather, it looked like an off-and-on style relationship with a few other romantic partners thrown in for good measure. It is unclear as to who was chasing who at various points of their relationship. If we are to believe Marcus, then she was chasing him. If we are to believe Tara's sister, then she was afraid of him. Why would you chase a man that you were afraid of? Something is not right here."

A few days later, Tara and Marcus would have another "heated argument" which she would tell one of her friends at her night class as well as another friend the next day while she had lunch.

According to Marcus, the argument centered around him breaking up with her. But Tara's sister Anita Gattis had a different story.

"They had a very bad argument," Anita said. "Several days before she went missing, concerning an 18-year-old that he was dating. My sister did not think that (the 18-year-old's) parents would approve of a 30-year-old dating an-18-year-old. I'm told that she threatened to tell the parents and they had a very heated argument over this."

Marcus said the argument was about something else entirely. He stated that she begged him not to end their relationship.

"She wanted me back and all," Marcus said. "And I said, 'I've started shopping outside of Ocilla, I think you need to do the same. Everybody in this town is connected to us one way or another."

"She approached me crying," Harper said as he repeated the same story on Greta Van Susteren's TV show. "She was very irrational, and she told me that if she found out I was dating someone, she would commit suicide."

But Tara's friend Osjha disputes the fact that Tara would do or say something like that.

"She's never said anything remotely similar to me ever any time."

Law enforcement authorities don't believe Tara committed suicide as she would have to go to extreme lengths to hide her own body and would have no motive to do so.

"There are a couple of contradictory things at play here," Orange said. "Tara was rumored to have dated some of her students so it would be hypocritical of her to criticize Marcus for dating someone in their teens. And it also doesn't make sense for her to come to Marcus' home begging to get back together. She had her share of suitors, some coming from out of town. She was a beautiful woman and she had options."

To her family's dismay, both the authorities and press would place Tara's life under a microscope. They had discovered that she had "several romantic relationships that occurred in relative proximity to one another."

"There was more rumors and innuendo," Orange said. "There were rumors that she was dating Rhett Roberts, her landlord's son. Rumors that she was dating one of her teenage students. Rumors that she was dating Heath Dyke, a police officer from another county. Even her own brother-in-law, Larry Gattis, was rumored to have an affair with Tara."

Both Larry and Tara's sisters are physicians. Larry specializes in geriatric medicine with only 3.3 out of 5-star reviews on Healthgrades. He was interrogated by investigators and expressed his outrage at the questions they were asking. One question was that if he had an affair with Tara and his response was judged by the polygraph as "deceptive."

ALL THAT AND A STALKER TOO...

Tara would have a stalker in a former student named Anthony Vickers. Friends recalled that Tara had taken special care to tutor Vickers but she later realized that the young man was "unstable."

"He was just kind of a troubled kid and that would be her nature," Osjha said.

Vickers was obsessed with his beauty queen teacher and claimed to have had a romantic relationship with her.

"She talked about the fact that he would call and he would rely on her and she knew it was getting too much for her," a friend named Maria said. "I just kept telling her, 'You know Tara, something's wrong."

Vickers was two years out of high school when he came to Tara's house and demanded to be let in. He pounded on the door until she called the police. Vickers resisted arrest but charges were later dropped and no restraining orders were ever filed.

The Vickers incident wasn't the only occasion that the former beauty pageant winner was being stalked. There was an incident where someone would call her home and make threats. The call was traced and it was determined to be a student in her homeroom who was promptly removed from the class.

THE NIGHT OF...

Before the night of her disappearance, Tara had enjoyed the company of her friend Dana and some teenage girls as they readied for the "Miss Georgia Sweet Potato" pageant. Her friend remembered

Tara as being in a great mood, helping out the girls with their hair and makeup. She would attend the pageant where she served as a backstage coach. Later that evening, she went to the house of a neighbor before going to a barbecue a few blocks from her home . Police believe that she had remained at the barbecue until 11 pm when she left to go home. They would find the clothes she wore at the cookout on her bedroom floor which indicated to police that she had, in fact, returned home.

From that point on, police "have no idea" what happened to Tara.

On October 24th, 2005, Tara did not show up to teach her class. Her colleagues called the police who showed up at her residence to do a welfare check. They would find her white Mitsubishi parked in the garage, unlocked. Upon entering her home, police found a business card lodged in her door.

There appeared to be no sign of forced entry. Searching through the house, police found her cell phone plugged into her charger. Her purse and keys could not be found.

Strangely, the clothes she wore the night before were piled on the bedroom floor.

Investigators found it odd that the car door was unlocked and that the car seat was pushed back. Tara was petite at only five-foot-three and would have kept the seat much closer to the steering wheel. They found an envelope of cash (one hundred dollars) on her dashboard while both her dog and cat were inside. Tara's sister said that she was an animal lover who would never just abandon her pets.

Something was wrong...

The police immediately called the Georgia Bureau of Investigation as the lacked the resources to pursue this kind of crime.

Taking over the case, the GBI believed that Tara may have left with someone that she knew, given the lack of a forced entry and the fact that only her purse and keys were missing. Neighbors did not report hearing any screaming at night.

Her disappearance shocked the small and close-knit community. To a person, Tara was described as someone who had a great personality, loved by faculty and students alike. Nothing in her professional life would suggest that she had any enemies.

Volunteers from the community immediately went to work. Irwin County students, teachers, and other townsfolk searched the area and put out flyers.

"Missing. Tara Grinstead. $20,000 Reward."

ROUNDING UP THE SUSPECTS

Longtime boyfriend Marcus Harper was one of the first to be questioned. He came with a ready-made alibi for the night of Tara's disappearance.

Marcus was seen at a bar with friends then went on a 'ride-along' with a former partner on the local police force. His whereabouts was "essentially substantiated" according to authorities.

Former student/stalker Anthony Vickers was questioned but later ruled out as a suspect. Like the others, however, he could not account for the entire thirty-four hour period when Tara was last seen and reported missing.

"Vickers is probably the only one I would rule out," Orange said. "This disappearance was too clean. Vickers was a disturbed twenty-year-old man with a crush. He would not have the emotional wherewithal or the knowledge to pull off a crime with no clues. But someone with law enforcement or medical training could."

But who left the business card behind at her door?

The card was left by Heath Dykes, a married Perry police officer with two children. He was from the next town over and had known Tara since high school.

Neighbors would tell investigators that he visited Tara's house often. It is unclear what their relationship was (outside of the obvious innuendo and rumors).

Still, he had left close to two dozen messages on Tara's answering message on the weekend she went missing.

There is small-town gossip that the two were having an affair. Local witnesses have confirmed that they saw his wife throw his clothes out on the front lawn. The content of the messages he left have not been made public but the rumors were that he was telling her "he was sorry" and that he "loved her."

What is clear is that he did call Tara's mother from the front yard and ask if she knew where Tara was and if she was alright.

Heath Dykes was the last known person at Tara's home that night as he arrived a little after midnight.

"There are simply too many secrets here," Orange said. "Something was clearly going on in Heath's mind in order for him to call Tara that many times over the course of one evening. One rumor is that they were having an affair and that she was going to tell his wife. So he was calling her in a desperate attempt to stop her from doing that. Another possibility was that she was calling him for help and he was returning her calls. His involvement led to a lot of outlandish speculation, one of which was that Heath knew that a hit man was coming for Tara and that he was calling to make sure that she was okay."

"I think the fact that she was beautiful and other people paid attention to her would obviously make some people jealous," Tara's friend Maria said. "I think she was afraid of the possibility of someone hurting her from being angry at her, having reactions to her dating people."

Numerous men were rounded up and questioned, there was Jim Perry who dated Tara years earlier, Rhett Roberts, Marcus Harper, Anthony Vickers, and Eric Cook among others.

Another unsubstantiated rumor that Tara was involved with another student named Eric Cook. A friend of his had made mention of their affair in an Internet forum post where he stated that everyone knew that they were "messing around." He also said that the police didn't make the information public out of respect for Tara's family as she dated around quite a bit. An alleged friend of Cook disputed the rumor on the forum, however. Cook would later die in a car accident.

A neighbor, Joe Poirier lived with his wife and was rumored to have been "obsessed" with Tara. The older couple admitted to "looking out for Tara" and they were fond of her. He was seen pouring concrete near his home the day after she disappeared.

Another person of interest was Larry Gattis, the brother-in-law of Tara. He was brought in for questioning after the disappearance. It would later be revealed that he had been asked if he had an affair with Tara.

Larry answered 'no'.

The polygraph machine marked it as a 'deceptive answer.'

48 HOURS

In 2008, Tara's case would be featured on the CBS News show "48 Hours Mystery." The show would illustrate the parallels between Tara's case and the disappearance of Jennifer Kesse who would go missing in Orlando, Florida three months later. The GBI would also reveal during the broadcast that they had found a latex glove in Tara's yard just a few feet away from her front porch.

The GBI forensic team would analyze the DNA left in the glove and determine that it was a man's DNA, they just do not know who it belongs to. They would compare the DNA samples of the numerous men who were associated with or knew Tara but none of them have matched.

The DNA has also been entered into the Georgia and national databases but no match has been made to date.

"The glove may be a red herring," Orange said. "Whoever entered the home left nothing behind, no prints, DNA, nothing. So it was obviously someone who knew exactly what they were doing. They wanted to harm Tara."

A HOAX AND FALSE TIPS

In February of 2009, a man calling himself the "Catch Me Killer" began posting videos boasting that he had murdered sixteen women. One of the women he described had a close resemblance to Tara Grinstead. The man producing the video digitally obscured his face and voice but police eventually identified the culprit as twenty-seven-year-old Andrew Haley.

Haley performed the videos as part of a bizarre hoax and was eliminated as a possible suspect.

Investigator Gary Rothwell has expressed his lament at how the rumors and speculation have caused unfair stress to many who have been already tried in the public eye. "Irresponsible public accusations have been made about them, and they have no way to respond or defend themselves. And it's frustrating that we don't have evidence to rule anyone in or out."

Rothwell admits, however, that he has information that has not been released.

In February of 2015, authorities acted on a tip which led them to drain a pond in Fitzgerald, Georgia.

They didn't go into details as to what the specifics of the tip were. The pond would be drained and nothing would be found.

ALIBIS

Police have alibis from all the men who knew Tara Grinstead but no one has been ruled out because no one can account for the full thirty-four hour period.

Rhett Reynolds stated he went to sleep after the cookout. Joe Poirier was with his wife next door.

The most elaborate alibi, however, came from Marcus Harper.

Again, Marcus was in a local bar and a friend of Tara's had spotted him there. She would call Tara at around 10:15 and 10:30 to tell Tara that Marcus was there.

After 1 am, Marcus left the bar and went to look for his police officer friend, Sgt. Sean Fletcher. Fletcher was on duty that night.

Fletcher knew Tara as well. Ironically, he was one of the officers who arrived at Tara's house when Anthony Vickers, Tara's former student, was banging on her door.

There were rumors that Tara didn't like Fletcher because he had told Harper that Tara was entertaining Heath Dykes at her home.

Fletcher would deny that speculation.

"What we can extrapolate from this scenario was that Vickers was angry that his crush, Tara, was with another man," Orange said. "So he goes to her home and demands that she talk to him. He's young, twenty-years-old, and doesn't understand why she would do this to him. He is then arrested by Fletcher who relays what Tara is doing to Marcus, a man that Tara is wary about because of his temper. So now we have more than just a love triangle, it is a love octagon, with numerous men vying for and getting jealous over the attention of Tara."

At around 1:49 am, Fletcher received a call from dispatch informing him that Marcus Harper was looking for him. The two met up and walked Fletcher's beat, checking doors in downtown Ocilla.

Around 2:45, Fletcher was dispatch to a home where a mentally unbalanced man, Bennie Merritt, had stumbled into a home and refused to leave. Marcus would join Fletcher on the call as did two other officers. Merritt, however, was gone from the premises.

Minutes later, they began to search for Merritt who was also a neighbor of Tara's. The drunken Merritt would accost the cashier at the local gas station then be apprehended. Both Fletcher and Harper had responded to the call at the gas station and by the time they were done it was 4:28 am.

Marcus then headed home.

Investigators would later be able to corroborate these details with multiple witnesses, including Merritt, who was scrutinized as a possible suspect in the kidnapping as well.

Marcus Harper, however, has not been ruled out as a potential person of interest in the case.

"Marcus's alibi is too perfect," GBI investigator Maurice Godwin said.

Both Larry and Anita Gattis believe that Marcus is the top suspect.

"He had the motive," Tara's sister said. "And the training."

The insinuation would draw the ire of Marcus who became upset that Anita consistently brought up his military and police training. He continues to deny any involvement in Tara's disappearance.

"I don't wanna hurt any innocent civilian much less someone I spent five and a half years of my life with."

"What is clear is that there isn't a whole lot forthcoming about Tara's personal life to draw the conclusions we need to about who is the most probable suspect," Orange said. "Like in the Natalee Holloway case, the sexual activity of the woman in question is kept hidden. If her background reveals that she was a promiscuous woman, there will e less sympathy and urgency to solve the crime. That is one of the more striking aspects of the case, aside from Tara's vanishing, is the cover-up of Tara's personal life in order to protect her reputation."

UNSOLVABLE CASE?

Tara Grinstead's case is still being investigated. The GBI reports that they receive numerous leads per day, most of which are false.

Her body has never been found but her impact on the lives of those around her and her students will never be forgotten.

"I'm so sorry to hear about what happened to Miss Grinstead," said Christine Kang, a South Korean exchange student from Grinstead's class. "She is so caring and giving to her students. I am sure she will come home soon safely. I will pray for her every night."

STALKED & ABDUCTED : THE TRUE STORY OF BRIANNA MAITLAND

KENDRA HICKS

There are approximately 2,300 United States citizens reported missing every single day. Some of these are runaways, some are misunderstandings, some are hurt or killed, and other just disappear without a trace. The friends and families they left behind are left with just a glimmer of hope that their loved one may one day turn up, which is oftentimes more painful than the closure of knowing your child or friend is in a better place.

Missing persons cases are a popular subject matter for shows like Criminal Minds or CSI: Crime Scene Investigation, but many real life cases don't end in the happily-ever-after seen on primetime. In the real world, these cases are often full of loose and dead ends, muddied by apathetic law enforcement or unclear communication between the victim and those close to them. Of those that go missing, the majority are women, who often present themselves as an easy target for those looking to inflict harm on another.

On March 19th, 2004, Brianna Maitland disappeared. The 17-year-old girl had just left the Black Lantern Inn in Montgomery, Vermont, where she washed dishes and occasionally served tables, when her car was found abandoned only twenty minutes later. Despite a brief visit from a local police officer, and curious passersby photographing the abandoned Oldsmobile, she was not reported missing for several days. Her parents, Bruce and Kelli Maitland, assumed she was at home, and Brianna's roommate was out of town at the time. Brianna left a trail of clues behind her, but over 12 years later there is still no official story for what happened that night. As the years pass without any major leads, the investigation has petered out and will soon be coming to a close.

Who Was Brianna Maitland?

Brianna Maitland was born and raised in Burlington, Vermont, where she spent the first seventeen years of her life living at her parents' quiet farmhouse. On her seventeenth birthday, she packed up her belongings and moved out on her own, despite her parent's pleas for her to stay another year. Her mother told interviewers that there was no serious issue or conflict that resulted in this decision, but that her daughter was fiercely independent and prematurely ready to venture into the world on her own. Although Brianna's early departure caused many to suspect an unhappy childhood or home life, she and her parents appeared to maintain a good, somewhat close relationship for the months after her move.

Brianna was an attractive girl, easily looking several years older than her young age. She was brunette and slightly petite, at 5 foot 4 inches and about one hundred and ten pounds. All around, she seemed to be a well-liked girl with many friends. Some rumors emerged after her disappearance regarding her moving to a new school district. These rumors blamed the move on Brianna being bullied relentlessly by other girls at her original high school, which motivated Brianna to pick up and move her life to an entirely different area. While these rumors are persistent, Brianna's parents or friends haven't confirmed them at this point.

At first, Brianna moved in with her boyfriend, James, wanting to be closer to a group of her friends that lived over 15 miles away from her parents' community. Moving in with her then-boyfriend seemed to be more a move of convenience than love; it didn't appear that she moved out of her parents' house with the intent of being closer and more codependent with him. She enrolled in a new high school, the same one as these friends, and began to settle into her new living situation. Unfortunately, her new home life was quickly uprooted by arguments with James, who she had accused in letters of having a severe drinking problem. By February 2004, barely a month before she would disappear without a trace, Brianna had dropped out of school and moved to a new house.

Now living with Jillian Stout, a friend she had known since early childhood, Brianna attempted to regain control of her life. The two young girls shared a modest home in Sheldon, Vermont, and seemed to be doing fairly well for themselves. Brianna enrolled herself in a high school equivalency program, hoping to earn her G.E.D. as soon as she would have earned her high school diploma if she had not dropped out. Brianna was reportedly excited about this test, looking forward to a new chapter of her newly independent life. Despite the hardships she had fallen on after moving from her parent's house, Brianna was determined to pull herself up and support herself on her own. Sadly, she would disappear only hours after finishing her exam.

While Brianna was not known as a serious troublemaker, she did drink and party like so many other teenagers do. At one of these parties, only three weeks before the night of her disappearance, Brianna was assaulted by another girl from her high school. At the hands of this girl, named Keallie Lacross, Brianna suffered a broken nose and concussion. Some rumors surrounding this attack suggest that Kaellie or one of her friends felt threatened by the pretty Brianna when she was seen talking to their boyfriend or a boy they were interested in. Although Brianna did press legal charges against Keallie, these were not yet resolved when she disappeared, so they were dropped several weeks later.

This scene cast light on some of the darker sides of Brianna's life. Her boyfriend was likely and alcoholic if not worse, she was bullied and harassed by other girls in her social circle who disliked her, and she likely partook in drugs and alcohol herself. While this isn't unusual for a 17-year-old, many in the community and police force expressed doubt that Brianna was attacked or hurt in some way. Instead, to them, she was just another burnt out, teenage runaway.

The Morning of Her Disappearance

The morning of Brianna's G.E.D. examination, she and her mother, Kellie Maitland, met for breakfast. Kellie reported that there was nothing out of the ordinary at this time, and that she had sent her daughter off to her test with plans to meet up and celebrate with her later.

For her celebration, Brianna chose to go shopping with her mother in the afternoon. Kellie said that shopping was one of her daughter's absolute favorite things to do. She said Brianna could walk into any store, pick the most "avant gard" piece off the rack, and model it like she was on an international runway. Brianna's sense of style was something her mother and many others admired about her. In television and print interviews, Kellie Maitland retells these memories with a clear fondness, holding onto those last final hours she spent with her daughter in 2004.

However, according to her mother, Brianna's shopping trip was cut short. As they were waiting in line to check out at one of her favorite stores, Kellie said that Brianna's attention was caught by something outside the store window. Saying that she would be right back, Brianna left the store. Kellie is unsure where he daughter actually went; she said that she never saw Brianna enter another storefront on the street. After paying for her items, Kellie exited the store and found Brianna waiting for her at their vehicle. She had no shopping bag from another store with her, and there was no one else nearby that Kellie thought she could have been speaking to.

There are many speculations as to what, or who, drew Brianna Maitland out of the store that morning. No matter what happened, Kellie said that her daughter was visibly upset the entire car-ride home. Wanting to respect her daughter's privacy, Kellie never asked Brianna what had happened earlier that afternoon, but this would be the last time she ever spoke to her beloved daughter. She dropped Brianna off in the driveway of her and Jillian's shared house, and then turned onto the highway to the quiet farmhouse she and Brianna had once both called home.

At home, Briana started getting ready for her Friday night shift at the Black Lantern Inn, one of the teenager's two minimum wage jobs. At around 3:30 in the afternoon, Brianna left her house in her 1985 Oldsmobile, leaving a note for Jillian assuring her that she would be back home after her shift was over. Jillian found the note when she arrived home, after Brianna had already left for the Inn, but then went away for the weekend without ever hearing from Brianna again.

The Last Known Sighting

The Black Lantern Inn, founded in 1803, closed its doors for good on March 29th, 2015. Remnants of the Inn's events and menus can still be found on Facebook and outdated travel sites. The most recent post on the Black Lantern Inn's Facebook page simply says, "The Black Lantern Inn is closed." The Inn offered an Irish restaurant and brewpub, which featured the Inn's own small batch beer brewed on location. Located in Montgomery, Vermont, a small town nestled between the East Coast's rolling mountains, the Black Lantern Inn drew a combination of loyal locals and transient tourists to its establishment. With a fireplace and public house feel, the restaurant and brewpub offered a cozy retreat for the perfect stag night or romantic getaway on a cold winter night. This is where Brianna Maitland spent her last documented hours.

Friday nights are notoriously busy in the restaurant and service industry, and March 19th, 2004, was no exception. In fact, it was even busier than expected, keeping the staff on their feet for the better part of the night and filling the back of house with dirty dishes and utensils. Backed up on her work, Brianna stayed several hours later than usual in order to finish washing the entirety of the night's dishes.

Sometime during the evening, Kellie and Bruce Maitland passed the Black Lantern Inn, hoping to stop in and visit Brianna at her new workplace. However, after seeing how busy the restaurant was, and not wanting to embarrass their daughter in front of her coworkers and boss, they continued on their way home. To this day, Kellie regrets not making that stop, if only to see her daughter one last time.

At 11:20 that night, the Inn's staff members were finally done with all of their closing duties. As per restaurant tradition, they all planned to hang out, have a drink, and relax after a hard night's work. Brianna, however, declined, stating that she needed to get to bed in time for her Saturday morning shift at her other job in nearby St. Albans, Vermont.

As far as Brianna's coworkers reported, she left alone from the Black Lantern Inn in her usual ride, her mother's hand-me-down Oldsmobile sedan. Brianna and Jillian's home was about twenty miles outside of Montgomery, but Brianna's vehicle didn't make it further than a mile from the Black Lantern Inn. And, as far as anyone knows, perhaps neither did Brianna.

Shortly after 11:30 that night, a man driving down Route 118 reported seeing a seemingly empty car parked at a run-down building, known as "the old Dutchburn house." He said the headlights were on, but he didn't notice anyone inside or near the exterior of the vehicle. A little after midnight, another report came in of a stopped car at the Dutchburn house, this time with a turn signal on. Later in the night, at about 4 a.m., an ex-boyfriend of Brianna Maitland noticed the vehicle parked off the road as well. Finally, early the next morning, a group of travelers stopped to examine the oddly abandoned vehicle, even going so far as to take photographs of the unusual scene.

A Delayed Investigation

Daylight revealed that the vehicle had actually been backed into the Dutchburn house, damaging the wooden exterior. By early afternoon on March 20th, a Vermont State Police officer finally arrived at the scene, deeming the car abandoned and having it towed to a local salvage lot. It wouldn't be until March 25th that the oddly abandoned car would be identified as Brianna's Oldsmobile.

Because of a series of unfortunate circumstances, no one noticed Brianna's absence until Tuesday, the 23rd, when Jillian called Kellie Maitland to ask if she had heard from Brianna. Since she was away all weekend, Jillian just assumed that Brianna had made other plans and had simply not returned home yet. It is unknown why her second job, which she was scheduled to work Saturday morning, did not question her absence. It's possible that they just thought she was another teenager pulling a no-call-no-show, too apathetic to formally quit.

As soon as Kellie heard that her daughter had been missing for several days, she began calling everyone she could think of. Despite trying to contact her friends, employers, and other family, Kellie failed to find any information on where Brianna could be. With no leads to go off of, she called the local police to file a missing persons report.

At this point, Brianna's Oldsmobile had been removed from the Dutchburn house almost five days ago. That Thursday, March 25th, Kellie and Bruce drove to the Vermont State Police in St. Albans to submit photos of Brianna with her report. It was then that an officer showed them the photos of the abandoned Oldsmobile on Route 118, and the Maitland's identified the vehicle as Brianna's.

As the news of Brianna's disappearance broke, questions began to emerge as to why the officer sent to investigate the Oldsmobile had not raised an earlier alarm. The Oldsmobile had been littered with all kinds of Brianna's personal belongs both within and outside of the vehicle, including: two uncashed paychecks, her purse, jewelry, spare change, a water bottle, and, perhaps strangest of all, a lime slice. Vomit, assumed to belong to Brianna, was also found in the car's front seat. News articles, personal bloggers, and other armchair detectives have accused the officer, seemingly unnamed in any public documents, of complete negligence when handling the Brianna Maitland case.

While the Vermont State Police conducted a several month long investigation, they held onto the belief that there was no foul play involved in Brianna's disappearance. The general consensus was that she had run away or been swept up in some kind of substance abuse. Brianna's friends and family continue to believe that she would not abandon her life and belongings like that.

In 2012, a young woman's skull was found on a Vermont highway, showing signs of age and being exposed to the elements for several years. While no conclusive evidence has been able to tie this discovery to Brianna or one of the other missing women in Vermont, it remains a possible sign of her fate.

Recently, on the twelfth anniversary of Brianna's disappearance, law enforcement revealed that they had collected DNA evidence from inside the abandoned Oldsmobile. It is unknown if this DNA solely belonged to Brianna, or if this was new evidence or had been collected during the initial investigation. There have been no public updates related to this potentially new evidence.

Brianna's family maintains a Facebook page dedicated to remembering her and encouraging others to come forward with information about her or other missing persons. Support for Brianna and her family continues to flow in through comments and pictures posted to the page.

Flurry of Theories

Unsolved mysteries, whether they be in the form of everyday murder or the paranormal, are a popular pastime for the average armchair detective. Brianna Maitland's case is no exception. There is no limit to the number of rumors and theories built up around her disappearance, some more believable than others. While there is no official statement on what actually happened to Brianna at this time, by breaking down the most prominent theories we can begin to understand what might have happened that night. While this list is not inclusive of every theory about Brianna's disappearance, it features the most likely or those that are most supported by the case's evidence.

A Drug Deal Gone Bad – One of the more common theories regarding Brianna's disappearance connects the scene of her abandoned car with the shopping incident reported by her mother. It is known that, like many girls her age, Brianna was often seen at parties where alcohol and other substances were being used. Whether Brianna had an issue with any particular drug is unknown, but it's very likely that she partook at least occasionally, and she regular hung out with teenagers who were known drug users and dealers. These facts lead many people, including some police officers, to believe that Brianna was caught up in a bad drug deal or otherwise got on the bad side of some of the area's dealers.

The most common story within this theory is that Brianna owed money to a local cocaine dealer, who she had been avoiding for some time. When out shopping with her mother earlier on the day of her disappearance, Brianna had spotted this dealer or one of their associates following her and her mother around town. This is when Brianna had gone outside, confronting the dealer and possibly promising to meet him later on with the money he was owed.

Later that night, either because the dealer was simply sick of waiting for his money or because Brianna attempted to avoid him once more, things turned violent. What happened after Brianna's car was abandoned is not entirely answered by this particular theory, but it is clear serious harm was done to Brianna Maitland that night or shortly after. Later, a story would emerge that filled out some of this theory's more gruesome details.

Murdered by Ramon Ryans – About three years after Brianna's disappearance, a police report from the Burlington Police Department offered to potentially solve the mystery. This report, given by Debbie Gorton, from Colchester, Vermont, claimed to answer the questions that the Maitland family and law enforcement had been asking for years.

Gorton's statement came about because her sister, Ellen Ducharme, had been charged with the drug-related murder of Ligia Collins. Some speculate that this story was an attempt to throw attention off of Gorton's son, who had recently been arrested for an unrelated crime, but that question remains unanswered.

In Gorton's statement, she claimed that Ducharme had told her about the murder and disposal of Brianna, committed by Ducharme and several of her associates. According to Ducharme, a known drug dealer, named Ramon Ryans, had taken a "couple thousand" dollars from Brianna which she had given him to buy crack cocaine. Brianna, either because she decided she needed the money for something else or because Ryans failed to deliver on the deal, confronted Ryans to ask for her money back. Ducharme told Gorton that Ryans had abducted Brianna on the night of March 19th, when her car was found abandoned.

Ducharme told Burlington police that Brianna was kept alive for up to a week, suffering who knows what kind of emotional and physical abuse at the hands of Ryans and his friends. Brianna was kept in Ryans basement, possibly even past the time of her death. According to Ducharme, Briann's body was dumped at an unknown local pig farm.

It is particularly strange, if this is truly what happened, why Brianna's attackers did not take her money or un-cashed paychecks from her vehicle. If her murder was motivated by money, these would be easy loot. More likely, though, this was a crime of pure rage.

Gorton believed that several people were involved in the murder and disposal of Brianna's body, including her sister, Ramon Ryans, Moses Robar, Darrel Robar, and Timothy Crews. No charges were ever made against these individuals in the case of Brianna's disappearance and the accusations remain uncorroborated by any local law enforcement.

Stalked at Work – It is sadly common for service industry staff, especially women, to be harassed and followed by their customers. While Brianna's primary role was in the back as a dishwasher, she occasionally served and helped out in the front of house when it was busy.

Another common theory of her disappearance is that she had acquired a stalker in her time at the restaurant, or from somewhere else who had then found her workplace and continued his stalking there. Since Brianna was an attractive, young girl, this theory is not too hard to believe.

Perhaps Brianna was aware of this stalker, though never confided in the police or her loved ones, and this is who she had seen outside the store she was shopping in with her mother. If she had confronted this man and demanded that he leave her alone, this would have made her nervous and on-edge like her mother later described. This rejection by his object of affection may have also sent the stalker into more violent methods.

With this theory, some believe that the man was hiding in her Oldsmobile's backseat, waiting for Brianna to clock out and head home. Shortly after she had left the Black Lantern Inn, he could have emerged and told her to either pull over or drive somewhere at his command. This also would have explained why the Oldsmobile was backed into the old Dutchburn house, because oftentimes women are instructed to drive into an object in order to stun or hurt an attacker in their vehicle. Unfortunately, if this is what happened, it appears that the stalker was successful in his pursuit of Brianna.

Pregnancy Scare – Fueled by the small town rumor mill, another frequently heard story is one of teenage pregnancy. Playing up Brianna's partying side, this theory suggests that a mistake between two young people turned into a case of cold-blooded murder.

On the day of her disappearance, Brianna already knew that she was pregnant. Maybe she had just found out, or maybe this fact had been weighing on her mind for weeks. Either way, when she left her mother in the store checkout line, Brianna was going out to tell someone about her pregnancy. Whether this was a friend or the potential child's father, Brianna did not want her mother to overhear the conversation and find out that she was pregnant.

Later that night, she had stopped at the old Dutchburn house. The vomit found in her vehicle leads some to believe that she got sick on her way home from work and pulled over in order to clean up or gather herself before continuing home. This is where someone met her, because she asked him or her to or because they had followed her from the Black Lantern Inn, most likely the potential child's father. Either way, this person was extremely unhappy at Brianna's news. Perhaps it was a cheating partner who had gotten Brianna pregnant, or simply a young man who was nowhere near ready for the financial and emotional responsibility of having a child.

The old Dutchburn house is backed by a nearby forest and river, which can be easily accessed by a short walk. If Brianna was killed at the location of her car, this is likely where her body was left. No trace of Brianna was ever found in this area, but there is always a chance that it was swept away or buried beneath the soil.

A Deadly Party – Following along with Brianna's supposed party girl image, this theory suggested that she had actually made it further than the old Dutchburn house that night. However, as we'll see, there are some discrepancies throughout this theory that make it highly unlikely.

After leaving for work that Friday, rather than going home to rest for her morning shift like she had told her coworkers, Brianna had driven out to a nearby party. Here she was either involuntarily drugged or willing took drugs herself. As the night progressed and intoxication levels increased, Brianna began to overdose. Unable or unwilling to get her the appropriate help in time, Brianna died that night at the party. Afraid of being caught, and potentially charged with the murder of Brianna, those at the party secretly disposed of the body. Later that night, her car was planted in order to look like it had been abandoned or that something had happened to her on the side of the road. If a couple drunk teenagers were driving Brianna's vehicle to the old Dutchburn house, this could also explain the vomit found in the passenger seat of her car.

The most obvious hole in this theory is the sightings of Brianna's parked car at the Dutchburn house less than an hour after she had clocked out of work at the Black Lantern Inn. This timeframe would leave her no time to get to a party, let alone overdose and have her vehicle planted by other partygoers. However, witness sightings are notoriously inaccurate, leading some to believe that the initial sighting of Brianna's Oldsmobile either didn't happen, was a different car pulled over on the side of the road entirely, or happened at a later hour and the witness was either mistaken or lied to the authorities.

For those who see Brianna as a wild, high school drop out who ended up hanging out with the wrong crowd, this story might be very easy to believe. Even law enforcement were quick to say that Brianna's disappearance was more likely an accident than premeditated foul play. Brianna's close friends and family don't believe this tale, though, and hold onto the belief that Brianna was an innocent victim the night of her disappearance.

A Victim of Human Trafficking – Human trafficking is an often overlooked issue in the United States, with many believing that it only occurs in foreign, third world countries in Asia or Europe. While most known cases of human trafficking occur at airports, large metropolitan areas, and other locations with a high volume of travellers and business, some do occur in small towns or seemingly innocuous places like coffee shops or malls.

Women are the most common victims of human trafficking, usually being sold into the non-consensual sex trade. While the men, or "Johns," who visit these women are rarely aware that the sex worker they are visiting is actually being held against their will, these women's captors can be violent, abusive, and frequently end up killings their prisoners. Some human traffickers will also force their victims to develop a drug addiction, often to heroin and other hard street drugs, so that they are more easily manipulated and apathetic to their situation.

Those who believe that Brianna, likely targeted because of her petite, non-threatening figure and good looks, was sold into sex trafficking believe that she was smuggled over the nearby Canadian border. This would explain why her personal belongings, such as I.D.

and jewelry, were left behind; the abductors would not want any identifiable information with her in case they were caught. However, it's strange that none of her money was taken if this was the case.

Final Blow From Kaellie Lacross – While Kaellie Lacross's, the girl who had attacked Brianna at a party just three weeks before her disappearance, charges were eventually dropped, she remained the primary suspect in many people's eyes. After all, it is quite possible that a grudge strong enough to assault someone over is a grudge strong enough to murder someone, purposely or not, over.

Whatever it is that triggered Kaellie's attack at the party, it's not impossible to believe that she wasn't satisfied with the outcome. If Kaellie was intending to teach Brianna a lesson, whether it was to not speak poorly or her or to stay away from particular boy, she might have felt the need to scare Brianna even further. Knowing that Brianna worked at the Black Lantern Inn, Kaellie could have followed her and forced her to pull over on the side of Route 118.

Here, Kaellie, likely the help of her peers, could have threatened Brianna and physically attacked her again. Whether this attack was meant to kill Brianna doesn't matter, only that it eventually did. Realizing that they had made a huge mistake, and would now be charged with not just assault but with murder as well, the group quickly disposed of her body. They could have placed the body in another vehicle, taking it to a different location, or carried her back into the secluded woods behind the old Dutchburn house.

If the motivation behind this attack was only to scare Brianna, then they would have had no interest in taking her money or other belongings. This theory is supported by having a clear motive, though there is no official report on what the conflict between Brianna and Kaellie was, and if it was serious enough that Kaellie would gone through the trouble of practically hunting Brianna down to resolve it.

The Mystery Remains

Despite this exhaustive list of theories, there is really no way of knowing what happened to Brianna until someone comes forward with new information. As the Maitland family and Montgomery community approach the thirteenth anniversary of Brianna's disappearance, there are plans to scale back the search for her and what happened.

Up until now, the Maitland family and Vermont State Police have funded a $20,000 reward fund for any information that leads to the discovery of Brianna Maitland, but after all these years with no solid leads, the plan is to donate the fund to a missing persons advocacy group sometime in 2017. Although the Maitland's have not given up hope, they are ready to take a step forward in grieving their daughter, no matter what has happened to her.

The Brianna Maitland Facebook page remains active, wishing followers happy holidays and posting alerts for other missing persons cases. Serving as a memory of Brianna, whether she remains alive or not, the page aims to draw out information on her case and the thousands of other missing persons cases that go unsolved every year. Brianna's case has also been featured on several true crime podcasts, television shows, and blogs, hoping to unearth the answers to questions that everyone has been asking since that cold night of March 19th, 2004.

www.ingramcontent.com/pod-product-compliance
Lightning Source LLC
Chambersburg PA
CBHW051839130726
47987CB00002B/608